Toddler Time

Toddler Time

150 Easy Ways to Keep Them Busy, Safe & Happy

Melissa Bogdany

Revell
Grand Rapids, Michigan

372 21
P
6

© 2004 by Melissa Bogdany

Published by Fleming H. Revell
a division of Baker Book House Company
P.O. Box 6287, Grand Rapids, MI 49516-6287
www.bakerbooks.com

Printed in the United States of America

Library of Congress Cataloging-in-Publication Data
Bogdany, Melissa, 1969–
     Toddler time : 150 easy ways to keep them busy, safe & happy / Melissa Bogdany.
          p.   cm.
     ISBN 0-8007-5886-2 (pbk.)
     1. Creative activities and seat work. 2. Toddlers—recreation. I. Title.
     LB1140.35.C74B63 2004
     372.21—dc22   2003026389

Contents

Acknowledgments

Many people deserve thanks for helping to put this book together. First, I want to thank my husband, Tim, from the bottom of my heart, for he made my dream of writing this book possible. Thank you, Tim, for giving me the opportunity to work from home and be with Emily. Also, thank you for all your ideas, which helped mold this book; for cooking and cleaning and all your help around the house, especially during the final days of writing; and for eating Papa John's pizza, Chinese takeout, and ready-to-eat grocery store chicken—all with a smile on your face. But most of all, thanks for making this and all my dreams come true.

Thank you, Emily, my precious little angel, for letting Mommy work while being with you (well, usually).

And thanks, Charlotte, for all your wonderful ideas and for being such a perfect big sister to Emily. You will make a great mother some day.

A special thanks to Summer Dorn and Lisa Santana, two great friends who helped watch Emily during my final days of writing. Thanks as well to all those who offered to do so.

I also want to show my utmost appreciation to all of my relatives and friends who, as parents themselves, contributed ideas for this book: my sister Deb Meier; my sisters-in-law Cindy Borr and Kelly Stoker; my mom, Shirley Stoker; and my friends Denise Bruder, Julie Daniel, Summer Dorn, Lynn Gilman, Stephanie Hockman, Elizabeth Kessler, Rene Leavitt, Kelli Robertson, Rhonda Sholar, Dawn Strickland, Dawn Volkema, and Susan Young.

I want to thank my mother, Shirley Stoker, and my father, Edward Stoker Jr., for always supporting and encouraging me in anything I have done. You inspire me to try to be my best.

Finally, I'd like to thank God for giving me my children and the opportunity to publish this book—they are all dreams come true.

Introduction

As I am writing this book, my three-and-a-half-year-old daughter, Emily, is climbing on my back, arms lovingly around my neck, attempting to put my hair in my eyes. This is why I chose to write this book. As a freelance writer and editor since her birth, I have found myself seeking creative ways to keep Emily occupied while I worked.

But this book will be useful not only to moms who work part time at home, but to all moms and dads. Any busy parents who need to cross things off their to-do list while looking after a toddler will find plenty of ideas here.

This book is not intended to be an end to all your problems. There's nothing magical about it. There's nothing that you can give your toddler to do that will keep him or her perfectly content for an extended period of time. Your toddler needs and wants your attention—that's how little boys and girls are made. And none of us should try to change that.

But this book will help make it easier for you to balance giving your toddler what he or she needs and still having some time to do what you need to do. It is intended to assist you in your busy life as a parent of a toddler or toddlers. It provides 150 quick, easy, inexpensive, educational, healthy, wholesome ideas to keep your little one busy while you get things done.

The ideas shy away from television programs and junk food. They mostly involve materials you probably have lying around the house. And these ideas can teach your toddler important skills and life lessons.

You may want to line up a few ideas for the same day. No single idea will keep your toddler occupied for hours. Toddlers have short attention spans and need new things to keep them interested. But if you can get bigger blocks of time with fewer interruptions, your day will be a lot easier and less stressful.

Which ideas will work best will depend on the child—and even the day. This book is intended to provide you with a variety of ideas so you can get moments of reprieve.

But when my daily to-do list leaves me in a state of panic that is only compounded by a toddler who doesn't see the need to cooperate, I simply try to remember what a blessing my children are. It is sometimes easier said than done. But when I am able to keep perspective and remember how wonderfully my children are made, the stress magically transforms into love. When your daily schedule gets difficult, I urge you to count your blessings. That's by far the best advice I can offer.

> Do not be anxious about anything, but in everything, by prayer and petition, with thanksgiving, present your requests to God. And the peace of God, which transcends all understanding, will guard your hearts and your minds in Christ Jesus.
>
> Philippians 4:6–7

Part I

Instant Ideas

Ideas That Require Virtually
No Preparation

1

What's Inside

Whether you work from your home or not, as sure as toddlers get into trouble, you have a lot to do—chores, meals, bills, and maybe even a part-time job. But if you're like most moms, you're often at a loss for ideas to keep your little one busy and out of trouble while you get your work done. This chapter provides numerous ideas on how to keep him or her occupied indoors.

Save old magazines, and let your toddler have at 'em.

Begin saving them now. The more magazines you have, the better. Your toddler will go through them quickly. Curious toddlers love flipping through the pages. Many magazines—even the ones you may think would be of no interest to a toddler—have pictures that little ones love to look at. Ads as well as editorial copy include interesting pictures. Magazines commonly feature pictures of water, babies, puppies and other animals, food, flowers, dolls, costumes, dresses, jewelry, just about every sport, airplanes, and so on. Obviously, you'll want to make sure the magazines are tasteful and the pictures suitable for your very observant toddler. A stack of old magazines can be a free way to keep your toddler occupied for a while. Your toddler may even find brochures and catalogs that come in the mail interesting. And since these magazines and catalogs are going in the trash, you don't have to worry about your child ripping the pages while you are busy with your task at hand.

Skills learned

By looking at pictures, your toddler can learn new words and what those items look like. For this to be a learning experience, you may have to peek over once in a while and point out a boat or an ocean scene shown in the magazine, for example. This also can reinforce words already learned.

Give your toddler a set of doubles when you get pictures developed.

Kids enjoy looking at pictures—especially of Mom, Dad, brothers and sisters—even themselves. So next time you drop off a roll of film to be developed, order double prints. A set of doubles is usually free or inexpensive. If you want to keep both prints of certain shots, take them out of the stack and give the rest of one set to your curious toddler. This will make him feel trusted with their care and included in an aspect of your life. Your little one will get excited to see the pictures, just as you do. The best part is that you won't have to worry about fingerprints or bends in the photos since you have a clean set of your own. You may even want to keep a special box in your child's room for the photos. You can put them away together when you are finished with your task.

Skills learned

Toddlers will begin to learn that pictures mimic real life. They will develop confidence by being able to identify individuals and objects in the photos. If you keep a photo box, your little one will learn to put things in their proper place when he has finished with them.

Stash a few new dollar-store toys, and pull them out when you have a busy day ahead of you.

Next time you're at a dollar store, buy a few toys or trinkets. Then pull one out when you need to sit down at your computer or get some ironing done. Something new should keep your toddler content and out of your hair for a while, although how much time it buys you depends on the child and the toy. Of course, you will need to swing by the store and purchase these toys when your child is not with you. Otherwise your observant toddler will see your purchases, and, for obvious reasons, the new toys will lose their effectiveness. Also, you will need to make sure they are safe for your toddler. This idea will only cost you a dollar a shot. Your time and sanity are worth much more.

Skills learned

What your toddler can learn will depend on the toy. Some of the possibilities: colors, shapes, and new words (names of objects).

Let your toddler dress up dolls or teddy bears in her own infant clothing.

Most little girls love dressing dolls. Boys also enjoy dressing up their bears or other stuffed animals. If you have saved your toddler's baby clothes, let your little one play with them. This will add excitement to the dress-up, and your toddler will discover what she wore as a little baby. This small clothing fits or comes close to fitting many dolls and teddy bears. You can leave a medley of clothes—shorts, jeans, sweaters, tanks, dresses, jackets, socks, whatever you have—in a box for your little one to pull out and discover. You could play along in a sense and still get your work done by creating scenarios for your toddler. For example, say, "Okay, your baby is going dancing. What is she going to wear?" Or, "If your bear goes to the park, what shirt should he wear?"

Skills learned

By dressing up bears or dolls, your little ones can learn a variety of skills, including how to put on certain articles of clothing, how to zip, how to snap, and how to button. In addition, they could learn what clothing is appropriate for different occasions. When your toddlers get old enough, they can practice tying shoes on bears or babies.

Give your toddler an assortment of buttons to play with.

If your toddler is old enough not to put things in his mouth, this can be a bundle of fun. Give him a bag of buttons that contains a variety of sizes, shapes, and colors. He can sort them by type, color, or size or just play with a handful of them. Your little one can line the buttons up in a row or make pictures such as smiley faces or shapes. Call it button art. If you are more trusting, you could spread some newspapers, get some glue and paper plates, and let your toddler make more permanent artwork that will be cute as a button. This idea works better with older toddlers. To ensure safety, you should be able to keep an eye on your little one when he handles small parts. When you are both finished with what you are doing, have your toddler help you put the unused buttons back in the bag.

Skills learned

Playing with buttons can help your toddler practice motor skills making pictures, learn shapes and colors, and recognize the need to pick up after an activity.

Put in home videos for your toddler to watch.

This is one time you might not mind your toddler's being glued to the tube. If you have taken recent footage with your camcorder, your toddler would love to watch it.

This can be exciting, stimulating, and interactive as your toddler recognizes the people and pets in the videos. Your little one will enjoy seeing her big brother or sister, grandma and grandpa, mom and dad, and herself! Your toddler will find it interesting to be able to see herself as a baby as well as what the people in the video were doing. Home videos can be a lot of fun and a nice alternative to watching a television program. You get the picture.

Skills learned

Your little ones will learn to recognize people, improving their memories. Your toddlers also will learn a little lesson in technology—that you can take pictures and watch them on television. Videos can stimulate language skills, as toddlers are likely to talk about the video and point out things they see—and maybe ask questions about them.

Have your toddler put pinecones in baskets to make home decor.

Take those pinecones your toddler helped you gather from your yard (or from somewhere else) and set out a couple of baskets. Have her arrange the pinecones in the baskets to make decorations to set throughout the house. If it's Christmastime, you could even have her arrange some small Christmas tree trimmings in with the pinecones. This will add color and a pine aroma in any room.

Craft stores and sometimes grocery stores sell cinnamon-scented pinecones and pinecones with a snowy look. As an added option, you may want to purchase some in addition to the ones you collect to improve the look and scent. You also could have your toddler add a couple of cinnamon sticks.

Crumble up a small amount of plastic foam and have your toddler sprinkle it on top of the finished product. Some of it will land on top, and some will seep through the cracks of the pine cones and look like snow. These baskets make gorgeous centerpieces or can be set on an end table, a bathroom or kitchen counter, or anywhere in the house. Your toddler may even want to give one to a grandparent.

Be very careful, then, how you live—not as unwise but as wise, making the most of every opportunity.

Ephesians 5:15–16

Skills learned

Your toddler will feel very proud to have made a centerpiece for your home. Activities such as this do wonders for your child's self-esteem—perhaps the best thing we can pass along to our children.

Give a bunch of shells to your toddler to play with and sort.

You may have shells in a dish or jar as home decor. If not, collect a bunch next time you go to the beach. Pull out any that you definitely don't want broken and give the rest to your toddler to play with. The sound they make when they clink together is soothing. Encourage your little one to sort them by type, size, or color or to pick out all the shells with holes through them. Little kids love sorting all kinds of things, so if you don't have shells, you can have your toddler sort something else from nature, such as fall leaves, which are fun to handle too because of the crumply sound they make.

You also could give your toddler a little bucket of water and have her rinse the shells and lay them on paper towels to dry. This will clean off any dust or sand.

Your toddler also can make a necklace by stringing the shells with holes.

Because of the beauty of these items from your environment, this activity naturally will occupy your toddler.

Skills learned

Your toddler will learn that many things in nature are alike and many are different. She can learn to compare like items while learning about colors, shapes, and sizes. She also will notice the differences between the types of shells or leaves.

Let your toddler fashion objects out of pipe cleaners.

Kids love to make things, and the freedom pipe cleaners affords them will be appealing. Show your toddler that they can be bent in any way, shape, or form. Briefly demonstrate to your toddler how to mold one of them into an object, such as a flower or a car, or even simple shapes. Then give a bunch of them to your little one and let him or her play and make whatever he or she wants. Just make sure your little one doesn't get hurt from the sharp ends.

You also may wind some of them around your finger or a pencil to create a spiral. Give these to your toddler to play with as well, showing him or her how to wind them together at the ends and make an animal such as a lion or a dog. It doesn't matter if your child's objects aren't identifiable; even abstract art will be beautiful to you and fun for your toddler to make.

Your toddler will form an attachment to these flexible figures.

Skills learned

Your toddler will improve his or her fine motor skills and learn how to create different items by molding pipe cleaners.

Tip

Stock up on arts and crafts supplies by giving them to your toddler for Christmas.

Have your toddler cut the ends off the green beans for dinner.

Start by washing your toddler's child safety scissors. Then show her how to cut both ends off each green bean. Have her put the ends of the beans in one plastic bowl, and the beans in another bowl or in a pan. Your smart little toddler will catch on quickly, so have her continue with the task independently. You may even set the bowls in front of the television and let your toddler do this while watching a movie. Be prepared and have patience, as not all the ends of the beans will end up neatly in the bowl; you may have to pick a few up off the floor.

When your toddler has finished preparing the beans, have her throw the ends in the trash. Then proceed to cook the beans while telling and showing your toddler the rest of the steps for preparing green beans for dinner, such as rinsing them off, putting them in a pot with some water, and cooking them.

When they are ready, transfer the beans from the pot to a bowl and let your toddler serve them to everyone. This will make her excited about and take ownership of the task.

A patient man has great understanding,
but a quick-tempered man displays folly.

Proverbs 14:29

Skills learned

Your toddler will learn how to help prepare a meal by cutting the ends off the green beans. She also will learn the whole process of cooking and serving them, in addition to feeling able to do it by herself.

Have your toddler draw and color pictures for a neighbor or nursing home resident.

Before you begin this activity, tell your toddler what you are doing, that he will be making a picture as a gift for someone in a nursing home or a neighbor, and that this person will love his artwork. Use blank card stock, a page out of a coloring book, construction paper, computer paper preprinted with a border or decoration—whatever your toddler wants. Give him a choice of a few different papers, if possible. Make it totally his project.

Have your child draw and/or color any picture he wishes to give. You may want to make a few suggestions of things to draw to get your toddler's imagination in gear. When your child is finished, help write his name on the artwork.

Then one day when you are not busy, give the art to your neighbor, or take it to a local nursing home and leave it for a resident or for a common area such as the cafeteria.

Be imitators of God, therefore, as dearly loved children and live a life of love, just as Christ loved us and gave himself up for us as a fragrant offering and sacrifice to God.

Ephesians 5:1–2

Skills learned

Creating art for a neighbor or nursing home resident will help your child learn the importance of giving, and he will feel good about brightening someone's day when his gift is delivered. Your child also will learn how rewarding it is to give for no special reason.

Have your toddler string jingle bells.

At Christmastime, give your toddler some yarn or string, along with some jingle bells (which can be found in different sizes in bags at a craft store). Have her string a number of them onto each piece of yarn. Shorter pieces can be hung from doorknobs or door knockers to make a jingle each time the door is opened. You can cut a large piece of yarn that can be tied and worn by your toddler as a necklace, and tie one short for a bracelet.

Your toddler also will enjoy shaking a strand of bells as she sings Christmas songs. She could make extra strings of bells to give to little friends.

This activity will be a fun way for your toddler to ring in the holiday season.

Skills learned

Stringing jingle bells will improve your toddler's hand-eye coordination as she puts the bells on a string as well as bring out the little musician in her.

Let your toddlers feed their babies with their own infant bottles.

Even as adults, we like to look back on our days as children. It's interesting to see what we did and what we liked when we were young. Your toddler will think so too. If you have saved everything your toddler has used or worn since she was a baby, dig out some of the bottles you used to feed her.

Give the bottles to your little one, perhaps even with some water inside. Help her set out all the dolls, babies, and baby paraphernalia. While she is playing with them, she can pretend to feed them with her very own baby bottles. If you can, also give her some of her bibs for the dolls. Your toddler will find it intriguing seeing things she used as a newborn.

You also may have your toddler wrap the babies in the same blankets you used to keep her newborn body warm and cozy.

Skills learned

Using her own bottles and blankets, your toddler will learn to nurture and care for little ones.

Tip

Planning a series of projects for your toddler will give you several blocks of time in which to accomplish things.

Open a snack to keep your toddler content at the grocery store.

If your toddler gets restless in the grocery store, you may want to resort to opening a snack, such as a box of crackers, and a juice box or bottle of water. Just don't forget to pay for the snack or drink when you get to the checkout line.

Since your toddler may be content when you first get to the store, wait until a few minutes into the shopping trip to open anything, then shop quickly and efficiently. Munching on a favorite snack (try to encourage good health too) will keep your little one from trying to toss everything into your shopping cart or from running wild in the store.

Try opening something new and different that your little one hasn't had before, such as bagel chips or sunflower seeds. The right snack just may be the recipe for success when shopping with your toddler.

Skills learned

By opening something at the grocery store, your toddler can experience new foods. She can learn about new food textures and flavors and her likes and dislikes.

Let your toddler cut pictures out of garage sale books.

Next time you stop by a garage sale, look for books with pictures. You can buy a book inexpensively—often for around a quarter—and your little one will enjoy cutting out the pictures with safety scissors.

The books don't have to be children's books, just ones with pictures your toddler would find interesting, such as cookbooks. And you don't have to worry about your child ruining the books because they cost you next to nothing. You may, however, want to make sure he understands that the other books in the house cannot be cut up (or hide the scissors). It would help to keep the cuttable books in a shoebox or other special place.

After the pictures are cut, they can be stored for future use for making collages or decorating cards.

Cutting garage sale books will begin a whole new chapter in your toddler's creative life.

Skills learned

Your child can improve hand-eye coordination and cutting on the picture outlines as well as learn about the objects he is cutting out, such as what the things look like and what colors they are.

Show your toddler how to make noodle necklaces.

If you have noodles with holes in them in your pantry and some string, yarn, or fishing line, you should be able to occupy your little one for a little while by letting her make a noodle necklace. You could make it a point to always have on hand noodles that can be strung.

Give your toddler some cut pieces of string, and pour some noodles into a bowl. It's as simple as that. You can wrap a piece of masking tape on the end of yarn to make it firm enough to thread through the noodles. (Make sure the string is long enough to fit over your toddler's head after you tie the ends together.)

Show or tell your child what to do, and she can take over until the string is filled. Then tie the two ends of the string together. The necklace can be for your toddler, for Mom, or for Grandma. Suggested noodle types are penne, mini penne, ditalini (short tube-like pasta), ziti, or rigatoni.

You can spend a little more time and make the project a lot more interesting by painting the noodles a couple of different colors the night before you use them.

Your toddler will have oodles of fun stringing noodles.

Skills learned

Your little one will get good practice with hand-eye coordination by putting the string through the noodles. She also will learn that having fun doesn't require expensive toys. Your toddler will treasure these memories when she grows up.

Have your toddler make art using dry foods.

Gather a variety of dry food items from your pantry—pretzels, Cheerios, noodles, fish-shaped crackers, nuts, sunflower seeds, waffle cone pieces, or the beans from fifteen-bean soup mix. Put some of each on a paper plate or in a plastic bowl for your toddler. Then give him some washable liquid school glue and a couple more paper plates and let him create designs and pictures by gluing the foods on a plate.

Picture ideas: Use elbow macaroni to make wavy water, fish crackers as fish under the water, and Cheerios or other round cereal as air bubbles coming from the fish. Or make a car using straight pretzels, forming the wheels with Cheerios. Make flowers using round cereal for the petals and straight pretzels for the stems.

You can help your toddler with this project before he begins by making a quick sketch of a picture that he can try to copy. Or you could glue your own picture using the foods, and your toddler can copy it.

This activity will be a fun treat for your toddler and is a way to put stale crackers and other snacks to good use.

Skills learned

Making art with dry foods will inspire your toddler's imagination and creativity by using objects in new and unusual ways.

Have your toddler pair up the socks in the clean laundry.

If you've ever folded laundry while your toddler was home and awake, she probably has unfolded much of what you folded. It's like taking two steps forward and one step back. If this is all too familiar, try this next time: Before you begin folding, pull out all the socks. (If you have a toddler, you probably have plenty of socks in the laundry!) Put all the socks in a pile and have your toddler match them up. After a quick demonstration, your little one may even be able to put them together and fold them in half. This helps you get your chore done (without getting undone) while giving your toddler something productive to do. Then you can put the clothes away, and Daddy will enjoy pulling a pair of socks folded toddler-style out of his drawer before work the next day.

> Train a child in the way he should go,
>   and when he is old he will not turn from it.
>
> Proverbs 22:6

Skills learned

By helping you fold the laundry, your toddler will gain confidence in her abilities—especially when Daddy says, "Good job!" when he gets his socks out—in addition to learning how to help care for your home.

Tip

Make contests out of some of the tasks your toddler helps you do. Maybe see how many socks your toddler can find in the pile of laundry, or give your little one a dime or quarter for her bank for every plastic container put away in the cupboard.

Let your toddler help you make a pancake breakfast.

Rather than keeping your toddler out of the kitchen while you prepare breakfast, involve him in the pancake-making process.

Have the ingredients where your child can reach them. Let him help you by cracking the eggs; pouring in the measured ingredients, such as the milk and dry pancake mix; and mixing the combined ingredients with a fork or whisk. Your little one could even scoop some batter with a ladle and drizzle it into the pan—under close parental supervision, of course.

Over time, your toddler will anticipate the order of ingredients to be mixed and look forward to his favorite parts of the process. You will accomplish a task, keep your toddler out of trouble, and teach him a few things in the process. Your toddler will really flip over the idea of cooking pancakes.

Skills learned

Letting your toddler help make a pancake breakfast will teach him patience while he waits for the pancakes to cook and a sense of accomplishment and importance from participating in a grown-up task. He also will learn some basic cooking skills, such as measuring and mixing.

Have your toddler make different faces on white paper plates.

Get a few cheap white paper plates, or cut some circles about the size of a face out of construction paper or card stock. Have your toddler make different faces on them using crayons or washable markers. You may even want to draw a few faces of differing emotions—such as happy, sad, and surprised—on a piece of paper for him or her to copy. Your child also can glue pieces of yarn or curling ribbon on for hair, a mustache, or a beard. Show your toddler how to glue a flat wooden craft stick vertically at the bottom of each face, with about an inch or two of stick overlapping onto the plate.

Later, when you're not busy, you may want to cut holes in the plate where your child's eyes line up and have your toddler hold each one up to his or her face in front of a mirror. Your toddler will be filled with joy expressing various emotions in a silly, unique, and creative way.

Skills learned

These paper plate faces will help your toddler learn about different emotions— and the facial expressions that go along with them—in addition to improving his or her drawing and artistic skills.

Give your toddler a bunch of buttons to string.

For this activity, your toddler needs to be beyond the stage of putting things in her mouth. If she is, it will be a fun activity to string buttons. You may have several in a sewing kit, craft box, or place where you saved all the extra buttons that come with your new shirts and other clothing.

A piece of string, dental floss, fishing line, or heavy-duty thread will work well. Fishing line may be easier for little fingers to work with, as it is stiffer. Give your toddler a piece of string about a foot long, and remember to tie a knot or button at one end before beginning this activity. After your toddler is finished stringing the buttons, tie a knot at the other end of the string, and you have a book or Bible marker that will be more special to you than any you can buy in a store. Or you can tie the ends together and make a button necklace. (Make sure the string is long enough before starting.)

Skills learned

Stringing buttons is very good for your toddler's hand-eye coordination and fine motor skills.

Let your toddler stamp envelopes while you are paying your bills.

Next time you're at the post office, buy several one-cent stamps. Think about it—you can get one hundred of them for only a dollar. Then, when you're writing out your bills, let your toddler "do bills" too. He can write on the stuffers that come with your bills, stuff them in envelopes, and stick the one-cent stamps on the envelopes.

Since little kids like doing grown-up things, your child will enjoy being like Mom (or Dad). And this way, you can keep an eye on your toddler; he won't be looking for a way to get into trouble in the other room. (I am convinced toddlers *look* for trouble.)

Do your bills together each month, and your little boy will begin to look forward to doing the task together. This makes an otherwise unpleasant task a special time for you too.

Skills learned

This activity will help your toddler begin to learn about the grown-up responsibility of paying bills— the process of writing them out, putting the checks in envelopes, and putting stamps on the envelopes. Go to the mailbox and mail them together to teach your child the final step.

Have your toddler help make homemade pizza.

You have to make dinner anyway, so why not choose something your toddler can help you do. Making homemade pizza is a good way to accomplish this since it is messy anyway—with or without your toddler. To save time, buy a ready-made pizza crust, and put it on a pan. Put some shredded mozzarella cheese in a bowl, some presliced pepperoni in another bowl, and whatever other ingredients you wish to have—each in its own, nonbreakable bowl. Scoop and spread the sauce onto the dough. Then give your toddler instructions and let him put all the ingredients on the pizza.

Meanwhile, you can be emptying the dishwasher, setting the table, or doing another job in the kitchen. When your toddler is finished with his or her "work of art," you can wipe the counter or table to clean any spills, and you're done.

While you're making dinner, your toddler likely is going to be creating a mess somewhere in the house, so he might as well be helping you and learning in the process. You will be surprised how much your little one will enjoy the pizza-making process, and he will hunger to do it again soon.

Skills learned

Your little one can learn how to make pizza and sprinkle the ingredients evenly on the dough. But, more importantly, the activity will raise your toddler's level of confidence as he or she gets to "do it all by myself."

Tip

By having your little one help with jobs around the house, you and your toddler can learn about his or her interests and talents, such as cooking.

Make a fort for your toddler using a sheet and chairs.

Kids love forts—anytime, anywhere. And one time and place to build one is in the living room when you are folding laundry. To keep your toddler occupied while you complete this task, grab a sheet from the clean clothes pile and drape it over two chairs set with their backs facing each other about three feet apart. To secure the sheets better, put a pillow on each chair.

While you are setting up the fort, have your toddler get some special stuffed animals, action figures, or other toys to bring inside.

Then while your toddler is playing, you can get the laundry folded. You are right there with her building not only a fort but a lasting memory. And it's these types of memories that your child will cherish for many years to come.

I have learned to be content whatever the circumstances. . . . I have learned the secret of being content in any and every situation, whether well fed or hungry, whether living in plenty or in want. I can do everything through him who gives me strength.

Philippians 4:11–13

Skills learned

Children can learn to use their imagination in deciding what they choose to do in their fort—whether they wish to set it up like a kitchen with plates and snacks or a bedroom with a pillow, blanket, play phone, and stuffed animals. Children also will learn to seek fun in ordinary things—not just in the latest toys—and to be content with what they have.

Let your toddler stick the bows on gifts at Christmastime.

We know how easy it is to spend too much money at Christmastime—not just on gifts but on all the wrapping paper, tape, ribbon, bows, tags, and gift bags you need for wrapping. However, many of these items can be found at a decent dollar store. So when you're getting your wrapping supplies there, grab an extra bag or two of bows or pick up a couple of bags half-price after Christmas for the following year. The bows will come in handy when you are wrapping gifts while attempting to keep your little one content and out of the way.

When it's time to wrap the presents, let your toddler attach one or two bows to each package all by himself. He also may stick a bunch of bows on a piece of poster board or cardboard as a holiday art project. It will be fun to notice any patterns that emerge. If your toddler cannot peel the paper off the stickers on the bows, you could do that and then set the bows upside down for him to use. Meanwhile, you can talk to your little one about Jesus' birthday.

Skills learned

Sticking bows on packages or making bow art with your toddler will help unwrap his creativity and teach him the art of wrapping gifts for the celebration.

Let your toddler help you clean with her own little spray bottle.

What? Someone's wanting to clean? Must be a misprint. Nope. Toddlers can be some of the best little helpers. They often want to be like their mom or dad, so take advantage of it while it lasts. Fill up a small spray bottle with water. (The bottles can be found with the plastic toiletry containers in many large discount stores.) When you have to clean the house, give the spray bottle with water and a rag, washcloth, or small sponge (you could cut one in half) to your toddler. She can spray surfaces and wipe them clean just as you do. This way, your little one is not trying to get into the cleaning supplies but still gets to help.

Even when it comes to such mundane tasks, treasure the time you can spend together with your little one. Letting your toddler help you clean will give you memories that will make these chores special to you, even when she has a home of her own to clean.

> Whatever you do, work at it with all your heart, as working for the Lord, not for men, since you know that you will receive an inheritance from the Lord as a reward. It is the Lord Christ you are serving.
>
> Colossians 3:23–24

Skills learned

This activity will help your child learn the importance of taking care of all your family's belongings as special gifts from God.

Have your toddler design gift bags.

Get out some brown or white lunch bags or solid-colored gift bags that your toddler can decorate. Solid-colored bags are available at craft stores, usually for less than a dollar. Lunch bags, of course, can be picked up at the grocery store. If you have patterned scissors, such as those used for memory books or scrapbooks, you could cut along the top edge of the bag to dress it up. A scalloped edge is nice, but any decorative edge will give the bag extra flare.

Your child can glue on foam craft shapes, pom-poms, felt, fabric, ribbon, tissue paper, construction paper, or other craft supplies you may have. He or she also may color on the bags. They can be made before a special occasion or anytime you need your own time, then stored until an occasion to use them arises. They can be used for friends' birthday gifts, Mother's or Father's Day gifts, a gift for Grandma or Grandpa, or whatever your toddler wants to use them for. And with the cost of patterned gift bags these days, you'll save money on this project that will have your toddler's personal touch.

Skills learned

Toddlers can learn to give to loved ones while feeling confident about their artistic abilities as they complete a project all by themselves. And that will be a great boost to a little one's self-esteem—a key element to carry your toddler through life.

Let your toddler draw at the counter while you make dinner.

Put a clip-on high chair onto a kitchen island, or pull a stool up to your kitchen counter or island (if it's safe) for your toddler. Tape a large piece of paper to the countertop, toss some crayons into a plastic bowl so they don't roll off the counter, and have your child draw pictures while you prepare dinner. Your toddler will enjoy being right there by you and seeing what you're doing. It's a whole new view for your little one, who probably has become all too familiar with the grain patterns in your lower kitchen cabinets. That in itself will keep your child's interest and curiosity. You also can encourage your toddler to try to draw the foods you are making for dinner—such as a tomato, a cucumber, a potato, or a strawberry. This is one activity that is sure to be appealing to your toddler.

Skills learned

Toddlers are like little sponges, ready to absorb anything you let them. By drawing while watching you prepare a meal, your toddler will learn a morsel or two while at the same time developing his creativity.

Let your toddler tear up the lettuce for the salad.

Your toddler likes getting her hands into everything. Well, this time, let her. When you are at the grocery store, be sure to buy whole lettuce leaves or heads, as opposed to the ready-made salads-in-a-bag. The former is usually about half or one-third the cost and a lot more fun for your toddler.

When it's time to make lunch or dinner, rinse the lettuce leaves and lay them on a couple of paper towels on the kitchen table to catch the drips. Then set out a large bowl. After helping your toddler wash her hands—you don't want a dirt- or Dial-flavored salad dressing—let her break up all the leaves into small pieces over the bowl. Your toddler will appreciate the chance to do the grown-up task, and she may develop a hunger to become the resident salad-maker.

We have different gifts, according to the grace given us. If a man's gift is . . . teaching, let him teach; if it is encouraging, let him encourage.

Romans 12:6–8

By doing this task, your toddler will learn how to rinse the leaves and rip them into small pieces to make a salad. She will get an idea of the work involved. Get different types of lettuce from time to time, and your little one also will learn to identify the kinds of lettuce. But perhaps most importantly, your child will gain confidence as you trust her to do the task independently.

Tip

Don't forget to reward and praise your precious little one every day for her help and accomplishments.

Let your toddler look at his own baby pictures.

Especially if your toddler is your first child, you probably have taken plenty of photographs during his first few years (probably even the first few days!). If this rings true for you, you have a few to spare. Pull out five, ten, or even fifteen of your toddler's baby pictures and give them to him. He will be fascinated by them. Tell your toddler who he resembles—"You have your daddy's hazel eyes." "You have your mommy's nose." Then let him browse through the photographs and look for the family resemblances.

Take the activity one step further—give your toddler some child safety scissors, and let him cut out the baby pictures. Then you may want to give your child a washable glue stick and a piece of card stock or construction paper, and let him glue down the pictures, similar to a scrapbook page.

If you have another child, let your toddler make a baby page of his sibling. Then your toddler can compare how they both looked as babies.

Skills learned

Your toddler will learn that people grow and change. He also will learn that God made each person different and unique.

Have your toddler string Cheerios or other round cereals.

At breakfast time, pour two bowls of Cheerios or other hoop-shaped cereal for your toddler—one bowl to eat and one to string. Cut a piece of yarn or string, and have your toddler make a necklace out of the cereal. It will be fun for your toddler to take a bite, string a couple of pieces of cereal, then take another bite. Make sure the string is long enough to fit over your toddler's head loosely when it's tied.

A Cheerios necklace can be practical too. Whether at the park, at the mall, or at home, your toddler will have a snack on hand (or on neck)—kind of like a candy necklace. Other loopy cereals—including Fruit Loops—also work well for this activity. To make the project a little more interesting, use both types of cereal. To make it more challenging for older toddlers, have yours string a pattern, such as five Cheerios, then one Fruit Loop, and so on.

This activity will whet your toddler's creative appetite.

Skills learned

By stringing cereal, your child will improve fine motor skills and hand-eye coordination while learning to be patient as the necklace slowly grows. Your toddler also will learn the important lesson of seeing the fruits of his or her labor.

Tip

Put a dab of glue from a hot glue gun on the end of a piece of yarn to help keep it from fraying and make it easier for your toddler to string things.

Let your toddler make PBJs for lunch.

There's something about PBJs and kids—the two go together, kind of like peanut butter and jelly. So don't fight this force of nature.

Instead, get out the peanut butter and jelly and some bread slices or hamburger buns. Also get out a couple of paper plates and a plastic knife.

Have your little one make peanut butter and jelly sandwiches for lunch. Inexperienced hands won't be able to prepare them as quickly as you could, of course, so this activity will free up a little block of time for you.

Meanwhile, you can be emptying the dishwasher, cleaning the oven, or sweeping the floor. You even could hop on the computer to answer a few e-mails or complete part of a task for work. Don't forget to come back to the table to share a PBJ lunch with your little one, who will be proud to serve you for a change.

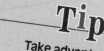

Tip

Take advantage of bits and pieces of uninterrupted time here and there throughout your day. Some days, that's all you'll get.

Skills learned

From preparing peanut butter and jelly sandwiches for lunch, your toddler not only will learn how to prepare a meal but also will gain confidence in her abilities once she completes the preparations alone.

Save scrap cardboard for your child to draw and color on.

One person's trash is another person's treasure. Such is the case with cardboard and your toddler. Ever notice your young toddler enjoying the box a new toy was packaged or shipped in more than the toy itself? Next time you get a box, don't be so quick to dispose of it.

Instead, cut squares and rectangles out of the boxes. Also save the cardboard on the backs of pads that you don't need anymore. Give the cardboard to your toddler to draw and color pictures on. He or she will like it because it is not flimsy like paper and is much easier to handle. Your child's little fingers can hold onto a piece of cardboard, and it isn't going to collapse like paper, even if your fidgety toddler wants to draw on his or her lap or lying down.

Furthermore, your toddler's pen or pencil won't puncture the cardboard. A piece of cardboard acts as paper and clipboard together.

Skills learned

By drawing on cardboard, your child will learn about the flexibility of different materials as well as how colors change when they are mixed with brown (if your cardboard is brown).

Give your toddler a few basic craft supplies, and let her imagination go wild.

It's just as easy to hand your toddler a few art supplies as it is to turn on the television or rewind a video and set out an unhealthy snack to appease her. And chances are, it's less expensive than buying or renting a video or buying treats to occupy your toddler. Give her some construction paper, colored card stock, or even scrap paper from your printer, along with a washable glue stick or some tape and a pair of child safety scissors. A large pad of construction paper costs about the same as a box of cookies or bag of chips—but it is a lot healthier, and it lasts longer.

The craft option just takes a little (very little) planning ahead to make sure you have a few supplies on hand.

Your child will enjoy just cutting, taping, and gluing the paper and making her own creations.

For quick and easy accessibility in the future, keep some colored paper, scissors, and a washable glue stick in a shoebox or small plastic storage bin out of your little one's reach that you can just grab when you need it.

Skills learned

Your little one can learn to cut, tape, and glue better as well as develop creative expression.

Get your toddler a new book instead of renting a video.

You've got a busy day planned. You need to do some work on the computer. How will you keep your toddler occupied? Most of us have thought, "I'll just pop in a movie."

Next time you're running errands and are tempted to stop by your neighborhood video store to rent or buy a movie to keep your toddler occupied while you get some work done, consider buying a new book, coloring book, or educational children's magazine instead. You can buy any one of these items for about the same price as renting a video. A book is a wise alternative, and it doesn't have to be returned in a few days.

If your toddler is with you at the store, let him or her pick out the book or magazine (within your parental parameters, of course). This way, you will know it's something your unpredictable little one will enjoy flipping through while "reading" the pictures. Then you can read the book to your toddler before bed that night.

Skills learned

Your child will learn to tell a story by following the pictures in a book. He or she also may recognize letters and small words. In addition, your little one will learn new words and how the words are depicted.

Give your toddler a piece of tape to play with and explore.

It should be a staple for your purse. You have your wallet, your pens, your makeup—and your roll of tape. Yes, tape.

Keep a roll in your purse at all times. Then when your toddler gets bored or out of control at the grocery store or if you have a lengthy wait at the doctor's office or you have a meeting to attend, toddler in tow, you can reach into your purse, pull out the tape, and tear off a piece for your toddler.

Tape is intriguing to little ones because it is unique and something they may not have played with before. Your little one will become quite attached to feeling the sticky tape with his fingers. It won't be as fun, however, if your child decides to try to stick it in his hair, so try to keep this from happening.

This goes to show that sometimes something as simple as a piece of tape can buy you that extra few minutes you need to get through the checkout line or have your name called by the nurse. Tape provides one sticky situation you won't mind your toddler being in.

Skills learned

Your child can learn about the sticky texture of tape as well as begin to appreciate and be content with the simple things in life.

Bring a pillow and a blanket with you to the grocery store.

A grocery store can be one of the most difficult places to take your little boy or girl. Toddlers don't understand why they can't have everything or why their parents won't let them have candy every time. They are just too young to grasp the concepts of money and good health.

But you can't always go shopping without your toddler. So one way to keep your little one from going nuts in the grocery store is to bring in a pillow and a favorite blanket. This will encourage your toddler to stay put longer. At the same time, hanging onto a blanket is probably more sanitary, as your child is not touching the grocery cart and contracting germs as much. Your toddler will find it fun to have a "bed" in the shopping cart. You even could drape a blanket over the top of the cart and make your child a fort. (You may not be able to put your groceries in the basket, but you can use the bottom shelf.)

Skills learned

As you praise your child for staying in the cart for you, good behavior prompted by the blanket and pillow, he or she can learn how to behave well at the store.

Involve your toddler in your decisions at the store.

Another way to keep your toddler tame at the grocery store is to involve her in your purchasing decisions. If a type of crackers, for instance, doesn't matter to you, let your toddler make the selection. Perhaps you'll ask, "Should we get rye (while holding up the rye bread) or pumpernickel bread (while showing that kind)?" You could give your toddler a choice of soups as you show her what each kind looks like. Ask your little one if she would rather get some Red Delicious apples or some Granny Smiths. Don't forget to point out each one as you talk about it. Also, you could buy something different once in a while to teach your child something new.

Becoming more flexible in your decisions at the store will teach your child and keep her attention focused where you want it. It's a healthy alternative to expecting an energetic toddler to simply sit and be good.

Skills learned

There's a lot to engrain into your precious little one's brain while at the grocery store—including identifying and differentiating between products and how to make healthy choices.

Have your toddler help put away clean dishes.

Use small children's enjoyment of sorting things and helping out by your side to your advantage from time to time. One way to do this is to have your toddler sort and put away all the clean silverware—no knives, of course—from the dishwasher or dish drainer. Have him put all the silverware in the appropriate slots.

Store your plastic containers where your toddler can reach them, and you also can have him put the clean plastic ware in the correct cupboard. Hand your child one container and say, "Put this in that cupboard," pointing to where it goes. Your little one will catch on fast and start grabbing the plastic containers from the dishwasher and putting them away independently.

With the right attitude (your toddler's will be patterned after yours), this can become a regular, enjoyable task together that provides crystal clear memories for you and your toddler.

Be joyful always.

1 Thessalonians 5:16

Skills learned

By having your toddler help you put (safe) dishes away, he is learning responsibility, how to help out with the chores, and how to sort things and put them in the appropriate places. Your toddler also will feel proud of his abilities. Meanwhile, your little one is not off somewhere else making another mess that will need cleaning up.

Let your toddler "help" decorate the Christmas tree.

The thought of decorating your Christmas tree and setting out the Christmas decorations with your toddler running around may make you want to catch the first flight out to the North Pole. Young children are bursting with energy and excitement that time of year, and something is bound to get broken. Next Christmas, one way to involve your toddler in all the fun and keep her away from the breakable ornaments and knick-knacks is to have her hang the mini ornaments made of wood, plastic, or other nonbreakable material. You can keep all of them together in a fun Christmas tin that perhaps someone gave you for a Christmas past. This then becomes your toddler's tin, and she can hang these ornaments. You even could set out your toddler's step stool to enable her to reach higher.

If you don't have mini nonbreakable ornaments, you may want to stock up right after Christmas when you can get a steep discount. These ornaments are perfect for little fingers to handle, and your toddler will have a ball helping decorate the tree.

Encourage the timid, help the weak, be patient with everyone.

1 Thessalonians 5:14

Skills learned

By helping decorate your Christmas tree, your toddler will enhance her fine motor skills, feel a sense of ownership in the family tradition, feel loved by being included, and feel trusted to help with the decorating.

Take stuffed animals, dolls, or action figures from room to room.

Take pillows, a blanket, a couple of towels, and stuffed animals, dolls, or action figures to each room in which you need to do work. Let your toddler set them up however he likes. Your child can create a slumber party by laying out a blanket and then the various stuffed animals, figures, or dolls on pillows and covering them up. Let your toddler use a few small towels or washcloths as blankets.

Grab a couple of books and encourage him to read them a bedtime story. Your toddler will enjoy feeling like the grown-up putting the toys to bed while being able to be near you—two things important to your precious one.

Just throw the towels and washcloths in the dirty laundry and have your toddler put the toys away when playtime is over. This activity does leave something else to pick up, but it can be quick and easy and well worth it if it keeps your toddler happy and occupied for a bit.

Skills learned

From this activity your toddler can learn about grown-up responsibilities as well as practice his own duties when it's time to clean up.

Play "I Spy" with your toddler.

Whether your schedule requires you to be in the car, at the store, or at the doctor's office, you don't always have the option of going alone. Often, especially in the case of stay-at-home moms or dads, you have your toddler in tow most everywhere you go. The problem is activities such as these are not at the top of your toddler's list of fun things to do. So what do you do?

The age-old game "I Spy" provides your little one with a fun element anywhere you have to go. Playing the game requires nothing. Simply think of something you can see, identify it by color, and have your toddler guess what it is. For example, if you're thinking of a yellow sign in your doctor's lobby, you would say, "I spy something yellow. What is it?" Reverse roles—let your toddler think of something he or she can see, and you guess what it is. Your observant little pride and joy will have fun spotting items anywhere—just wait and see.

Skills learned

By playing "I Spy," your toddler will sharpen his or her eye while also learning new objects and identifying colors.

Let your toddler play with packing popcorn.

When a package arrives in the mail, if your toddler is like most little ones, she immediately begins playing with the packing popcorn in the box. There's something irresistible about packing popcorn. But as parents, we usually tell our toddlers, "No, no," in an attempt to avoid the appearance of a blizzard in our living rooms.

Sometimes, however, when you really need to accomplish something without a lot of interruptions, a little mess is worth it. Anyway, messes usually look much worse than they are. So don't throw away—but store away—that packing popcorn for a special time. Then pull it out for your toddler to play with. She may even break up the pieces over the top of decorative baskets filled with pinecones for a snowy effect. (See idea 7 on using pinecones as decor.) Just make sure your little one doesn't eat this popcorn.

When you are free from your tasks, just take a minute or two to sweep or vacuum up the remains.

Skills learned

Your toddler can learn about the texture of the foam and its qualities—such as its light weight, break-ability, and squeaky sound—as she feels it and breaks it up.

Keep some small toys in your purse at all times.

You never know when your toddler will get bored or fidgety or where you'll be. To prevent boredom as best you can, keep a few small toys in your purse or tote bag so you will have them wherever you go. Restaurants' kids meal toys are convenient and often small enough. Other toys that are good for stashing include miniature plush toys and dolls. Don't forget to keep a few crayons and a small notebook or sticky pad in your purse too.

Then, whether you're at an appointment, in the car, or in line at the bank or grocery store, you'll be able to buy yourself a little bit of time while your toddler plays with the toys or colors pictures. Rotate the toys once in a while, and soon your toddler will become curious about what you have to play with and may even look forward to those previously dreaded errands.

Skills learned

Your toddler will learn that moms or dads are prepared and will do whatever it takes to take care of their precious little ones.

Try to spot certain things on car rides.

If you're on a long trip or have to run a lot of errands one day, an idea that will help occupy your toddler and take his or her mind off the lengthy ride is to look for a certain object, such as water towers, that will be visible over and over in your travels.

Other objects you and your toddler could try to spot include billboards, semi trucks, certain types of fruit trees, flowers, or tall buildings. Encourage your little one to try to see how many of them he or she can find by the time you reach your next destination. Get your toddler involved, and ask him or her what you could hunt for next. Your little one will enjoy playing the game; it will lead him or her down the road to contentment.

Skills learned

By looking for particular objects out on the road, your toddler can learn new objects, what they look like, and how the same objects differ from one another in their uniqueness.

Have your toddler make houses with wooden craft sticks.

Save the sticks from Popsicles or other frozen treats. And when you accumulate a bunch of them, give them to your toddler along with some washable liquid school glue. Lay out some newspaper on the table and show her how to glue them together by stacking them and overlapping the edges to make a house. Your toddler can make different sizes and shapes of houses on other occasions until she has created a small village. If this is too difficult for your young toddler, just let her glue the sticks together in any abstract way she would like.

For additional sticks, try your local dollar store. Some dollar stores sell packs of two or three hundred—a bargain at twice the price if they help keep your little one occupied for a while. You can even get colored sticks for added beauty and excitement.

Skills learned

Constructing with craft sticks will teach your toddler how to put something together one piece at a time. If your little one sticks to it, she will watch her project get bigger and bigger with each new piece. These early building skills will act as a solid foundation for your toddler to build upon.

Tip

If you're working at home, it's worth spending a dollar or two on an item at the store to keep your toddler busy and enable you to have a job and earn money.

Have your toddler help you make homemade noodles.

Following a recipe for homemade noodles such as the one below, show your toddler how to cut small pieces of prepared dough to make little noodles. Then let him continue cutting the noodles until the dough is gone or he becomes restless. As your toddler helps you make dinner, his excitement is sure to be kicked up a notch.

Ingredients:
1 cup flour
¼ teaspoon salt
1 egg, slightly beaten
¼ cup milk
1 49½ ounce can chicken broth

In a medium-sized bowl, mix flour, salt, and beaten egg gently with a fork. Add milk and stir with a fork until blended. Let the dough rest for 10 minutes. Meanwhile, sprinkle flour on about 12 square inches on the countertop. Lift the dough out of the bowl. If it feels sticky, pat it on the flour and shape it into a ball. Place it on the floured area and roll it out until it is about ¼ inch thick. (When rolling out the dough, always place the rolling pin in the center and roll in an outward motion. After each roll out, flip the dough over. Keep the dough dry by sprinkling flour on as you lift the dough out of the bowl as well as after you flip the dough over each time.)

Begin at the edge nearest you and roll the dough up in a single long roll. If you find a sticky spot, sprinkle a little flour on it.

Cut the rolled dough into strips about ¼-inch wide. Gently unroll each strip and lay it out on the floured work area. Allow it to dry for 90 minutes on one side, and then turn over each strip for another 30 minutes.

Have your toddler help cut the long strips into the noodle length you desire. Show your little one how to cut some noodles using a plastic knife.

Then boil the chicken broth in a large pot. Carefully drop the noodles into the broth. When the broth has returned to a boil, reduce heat to low (or until it is bubbling slowly) and simmer uncovered for an hour. Stir occasionally.

When the noodles are ready, put them into a bowl and have your toddler scoop them onto plates for dinner (recipe serves four).

Skills learned

From helping to make noodles, your toddler can learn how to prepare the meal, practice motor skills serving the noodles, and gain responsibility in helping to make dinner.

Teach your toddler a new song.

Whether you are folding laundry, doing the dishes, trimming bushes, or driving in the car, sing with and to your toddler. Singing will keep your little one's attention while you cross tasks off your to-do list. This idea, of course, works best when you don't have to concentrate deeply. And by now, with a toddler, you certainly have learned to do more than one thing at a time.

Sing a favorite song together, or teach your toddler a new song. Try new ways of singing a song, such as taking turns singing every other line in a familiar song. It then becomes like a game. Adding a different twist to something ordinary is sometimes enough to capture a toddler's interest. You also may want to add music. Even throw in a dance move here and there. These things will liven up this activity and make it a fun time for your toddler. With a little rhythm from time to time, both you and your toddler will end your day on a high note.

Skills learned

By singing with your toddler, he or she will learn new words and new songs and how to imitate different pitches.

Get help watching your toddler from a friend.

There will be days when no matter what you do, your precious little one will want nothing but your attention. And these days are not predictable. Therefore, when you know you are going to have a very busy day, you may want to see if a friend of yours who also has small children can watch your toddler for a while.

This way, your child is having a fun day playing with another child, and you are getting work done without interruptions or messes to clean up. This is a win-win situation for you and your toddler—perhaps not for your friend, but she will have her day when your schedule calms down and you return the favor. Swapping kids now and then saves you from having to pay a babysitter when you need one the most. And both your toddler and your friend's will enjoy having a playmate for two days while each grown-up gets things accomplished.

Take this idea one step further, and you and a few of your friends can take turns watching one another's children on Friday or Saturday evenings while the others enjoy a date night with their spouses.

Skills learned

Your child can learn from being around other children who are at different levels of learning and who have had different experiences that have molded their realm of knowledge.

When you have a lot of errands to run, bring a bag of books along.

When you have running around to do and you will have your toddler with you, bring some books along for the ride. Pack a bunch of them in a backpack or tote bag. The more books, the better, when it comes to keeping your little one's interest. Variety is key with toddlers, whose attention spans sometimes are shorter than their pinky toes. When one book becomes boring or one you think your toddler will love gets chucked onto the floor of your minivan, he or she will have many more from which to choose.

A bag of books will be helpful in the car, at the doctor's office, or at the salon. Make sure to include your toddler's favorite titles in the mix.

Blessed is the man who finds wisdom,
the man who gains understanding.

Proverbs 3:13

Skills learned

By going through his or her books, especially familiar ones, your toddler will learn to "read" the pictures and follow along. This will improve your child's ability to identify pictures, and he or she may begin to recognize some words. Pages can be written about the endless benefits books can bring.

Pop in an exercise video for your toddler to move along to.

Whether you are exercising or trying to get something else accomplished, your toddler may find an exercise or stretching video interesting. So put on the video and let your little one gently go through the motions. You could set out your exercise mat for your toddler to use to make him more comfortable. Low-impact exercises may be a good option. Your toddler will have fun marching along in place, trying jumping jacks, and doing knee lifts. But be careful that your child doesn't try anything too strenuous. You may want to stretch together before starting the video.

This activity not only will be fun for your toddler, but he will be able to release some of that endless toddler energy. Your little one will jump at the chance to follow along with an exercise video.

Skills learned

Your toddler will learn basic exercise motions and that it is important to his body's health to get regular exercise—and stretch first. Your child also will practice and improve his balance and coordination as he attempts to wave his arms while marching in place, for example.

Give your toddler a poster board on which to color a mural.

Murals are appealing to create and to look at because they are so big. So give your toddler a poster board or very large piece of white paper, along with some crayons and washable markers, and let her get to work designing anything she wants.

Your toddler will be blown away by the sheer size of the art project. And poster boards can be purchased at many grocery stores, as well as craft stores, for under 50 cents apiece. While they come in multiple colors, get white for the best coloring results. This giant art project should be a huge success in captivating your toddler's attention. And you will have a beautiful piece of your child's artwork to show.

Skills learned

By coloring a large picture on a poster board, your toddler can begin to learn about proportions—making pictures of people larger on a poster board than on a small sheet of paper—while fine-tuning the fine art skills of your little artist.

Tip

Don't overcommit on your responsibilities for a day when you have a toddler around. This will create stress, and it will be harder for you to have patience with your little one. Schedule time for breaks with your toddler.

Have your toddler sort whites and colors in the laundry.

When you've had a busy week, with a husband and possibly older children playing sports and a toddler being a toddler, your laundry basket looks like Mount St. Helens in no time. You've ignored it all you can, and finally you can't stand it. You take little breaks from your schedule and wash, wash, wash the laundry like a machine. Then you dry, dry, dry.

Now it's clean and dry, but you've got that deadline to meet or that task to accomplish before the end of the day, so you switch gears from the laundry. But you still have Mount St. Helens in your home; it's just clean now. You may not have thought about using this to your advantage, but it can keep your little one busy for some time while you do what you need to do. Have your toddler separate all the colored items from the white items. Set out a basket for each, or simply start two piles. This activity can be done in any room of the house—just put the laundry near where you need to be. This type of sorting will enable you to focus on your task at hand with minimal interruptions.

Skills learned

By sorting colors from whites in the laundry, your little one will learn colors as well as how to identify similar and dissimilar items.

Pick up a pack of stickers at the store.

Little kids love to play with stickers. So a new package of stickers with interesting pictures will make a good impression on your toddler. You can buy them while you are at the grocery store, and they generally cost just a little more than $1.50 for four sheets. The money is worth it if it enables you to work and bring in income. But if you don't want to spend the extra money, you could find something in your shopping cart that you don't need, put it back, and get the stickers instead.

Don't spoil the surprise by showing the stickers to your toddler. Save them and pull them out when you need some time with minimal interruptions. If your little one sees them when you buy them, she will want them right away. It's the surprise when she first sees them that will capture your child's attention and make her attached to the stickers for a while.

You can give your toddler some computer paper, construction paper, or card stock on which to stick the stickers. Fold the paper in half, and it can become a card. Some crayons will give your toddler even more creative possibilities.

Skills learned

Your toddler will improve her hand-eye coordination as she attempts to stick the stickers straight on the paper. Your child also will enhance her creativity.

Show your toddler how to "draw" with yarn on felt.

Take a piece of felt (about twenty cents apiece at a craft store), and glue it with a hot glue gun or other glue onto a piece of cardboard. If possible, use felt that is your toddler's favorite color. Then cut several small pieces of yarn, and put them in a plastic container. Cut different lengths and colors—the bigger the variety, the better.

Then sometime when you need to be busy, no matter where you are (at home, in the car, at an appointment), give the felt board and yarn to your toddler. Show him how to draw pictures simply by putting the yarn on the felt, then let your little one take over and express his own creativity. Your little one may want you to look at his drawings from time to time, but he will be content making yarn designs. He can make one after the other simply by pulling up the yarn and starting over again. And with the light weight of the board and yarn, your toddler will want to go back to the drawing board frequently.

Skills learned

Your toddler will learn new ways to express creativity by "drawing" pictures and designs with yarn.

Have your toddler unload the canned and boxed goods in the groceries.

You've accomplished the grocery shopping with your toddler, sometimes no small feat in itself. Now you have a lot of other things left on your to-do list at home—work, chores, dinner. Why not get some help from your little one?

Have her put all the cans and boxes away in the pantry. To do this, though, you should store these items on the lower shelves where she can reach. Also, store items that could be messy (such as flour) and harmful (such as cooking spray and plastic bags) up high so your toddler won't get into them while putting groceries away.

Your child will be happy to help out—stacking cans and boxes will be like building with blocks—and will take a sense of ownership in being able to put them away in the order she likes. You'll have to be willing to accept a less-than-perfect pantry, but if you do, you will save time by having a helper and by not having to clean up a mess your toddler otherwise would be off making somewhere else in your house. And you'll have more time to get things accomplished.

Skills learned

Helping put the groceries away will teach your toddler responsibility, as well as balance, as she puts the boxes and cans in order.

Let your toddler play with your hair accessories.

Get out your curlers, headbands, hair clips, elastic bands, a comb, a brush, and other hair accessories. Set the items and your toddler in front of a mirror, and let your little girl play with them and practice doing her hair. No heated curlers, of course. She also may want to practice on her dolls' hair. If you have a handheld mirror, give that to your little girl too. (Make sure there is a rug beneath her, though.) Show her how to look at the hair on the back of her head using the two mirrors. This may be a new, fascinating concept for your little one.

Since little girls love playing with hair, this activity is sure to keep your toddler out of any hairy situations for a while. Combine this activity with playing dress-up (see idea 91), and you may double your toddler's pleasure.

Skills learned

Even fun activities such as practicing putting hair accessories in her own and her dolls' hair will help your little girl learn to enhance her fine motor skills while learning how to part, brush, and care for hair. She also can learn how mirrors work by using one aimed into another to see the back of her head.

Give your toddler his own kitchen cupboard.

Select one lower cupboard in your kitchen where your toddler will be least in your way if he is playing near it. Keep only nonbreakable items in that cupboard—including plastic bowls, containers and lids, and your toddler's plastic plates, bowls, and cups. Plastic thermoses, foam can coolers, and a couple of wooden spoons for your toddler's experimental purposes also could go well there.

Let this become your little one's cupboard. Allow him to open it and play with the items inside whenever he wants—but especially while you do work in the kitchen, whether it is doing dishes, making dinner, or doing paperwork at your kitchen table.

Your little one will enjoy sorting, stacking, and lining up the containers. He also may make music by tapping on the containers as if they were drums or by banging two items together. A cupboard of his own is sure to keep a lid on your toddler's boredom, giving you a few minutes to accomplish a task.

Skills learned

Your toddler will learn which items fit inside others, gain practice building with and stacking the items, and get an understanding of what different materials feel like and sound like when tapped (okay, more likely pounded) against other items.

Have your toddler serve up pretend meals.

Gathering a few things from your kitchen so your toddler can pretend to cook can serve you well when you have a lot on your plate. The proof is in the pudding.

Give your little one an apron, along with a pencil and paper, to take orders. Pull out an old oven mitt, a small pan, some plastic picnic plates, and some old place mats. You also may buy some place mats on clearance for as little as a quarter apiece. Use plastic pretend food to make the meal complete. Many toddlers already have plastic play food, but if you wanted to get some, a large container of it is inexpensive.

Your little one will have fun acting as waiter or waitress and cook at the same time. And when your toddler is cooking up pretend meals, you can put interruptions on the back burner.

Skills learned

This activity will teach your toddler how to set the table and how to cook without getting burned.

73

Give your toddler a small notebook and a few crayons to draw with in the car.

Keep a small spiral notebook or a sticky pad in your car. Small notebooks are easy for little hands to hold. Also, keep a few crayons in your purse—but don't leave them in the car because they will melt and make a big mess if it gets hot enough in your car. When you get your toddler out of the car, remember to remove the crayons as well. You will want to carry washable crayons so any stray crayon marks can be removed from the material in your car.

Then when your little one becomes ornery on car rides, pull out the pad and crayons and give them to your child to draw pictures or just make colorful scribbles. Your little boy or girl may be able to draw pictures of things he or she sees out the car window, such as trees, birds, cows, flowers, school buses, and houses. With this activity, you should see a marked improvement in your precious little one.

Skills learned

Your toddler will improve his or her drawing skills and learn to identify different objects as you point out new things while driving and suggest your little one try to draw them.

2

Out and About

Need to get tasks accomplished outdoors? From getting your little one involved in helping you wash your car to getting help with the yard work to finger painting with yogurt, this chapter provides instant ideas that will keep your little one occupied while you have to be outside.

Write out your bills while your toddler plays at the nearest park.

What child doesn't like the park? If you need to spend thirty minutes or an hour making out your bills, why not take your child—and your bills—to a nearby park (weather permitting, of course). This way, your toddler won't be battling for your attention when you need to concentrate and be accurate. This is also a good solution when you need to balance your checkbook, fill out invitations, or write thank-you cards. Just remember to keep an eye on your toddler whenever you're at the park. If there is a fenced-in park near you, that would be all the more helpful. You wouldn't have to worry about your child running out into the road. A morning running and playing is healthy for your toddler and is sure to spark his or her enthusiasm while you accomplish these tasks.

Skills learned

Your toddler can learn a lot at the park—including how to use the different equipment on the playground, coordination from using the equipment, the importance of taking turns with other children, and social skills as he or she intermingles with other kids on the playground.

Get your toddler involved with washing your car.

Prepare a separate little bucket of soap and water and get a rag or sponge that is small enough for little hands to work with. You could even use a plastic sand pail. Dress your toddler—and yourself—in a bathing suit or clothes that you don't mind getting wet and dirty.

Let him spray the hose and wipe the lower areas of your car. You'll want to make sure you have the right kind of nozzle on your hose. The best kind for kids is the old-fashioned, screw nozzle. This enables you to adjust the water pressure to a slow, constant level. If possible, steer clear of giving your toddler a trigger nozzle because it's usually too hard for small fingers to squeeze. And if they can squeeze it, the water pressure will be too powerful for your little one to handle. If that's all you have, there usually is an adjustment on the back of the nozzle so you can reduce the water flow.

When you're done washing, you can give your toddler a washcloth instead of a big towel to help you dry the car.

Skills learned

By helping wash the car, your child will learn to take care of his things and recognize that his things are really God's possessions, which deserve the best care. Your little one also will learn confidence in his abilities— especially if you don't let him see you get his missed spots! Your child will love to help. (Kids love doing anything involving water.) You can praise him for a job well done.

Tip

Don't assume your little boy or girl is too young or small to help you out with tasks. Your toddler just may surprise you with how helpful he or she can be, given the chance.

77

Take your toddler with you when you fill the bird feeder.

Before you grab the bird seed, grab your toddler. Take her when you get out the seed and say, "This is what birds eat. Let's put out the bird seed." Then go outside and show your toddler how to feed the birds in your yard.

Remember, your toddler is much shorter than you are. So if you can, take the bird feeder down while you fill it so your little one can see what you are doing. Get a funnel, and your toddler can hold it while you pour the bird seed into it.

Then after you put the feeder back in its place, wait a few moments (or come back later) and see if any birds come by to nibble. Seeing birds eat what you put out for them will help the process come together for your toddler.

Skills learned

Your toddler will learn what's involved with feeding the birds. She also will learn that bird seed is not for people but for birds. Even at a young age, your child can develop not only a love of nature but also a hunger to care for God's creatures.

Let your toddler help you water the flower or vegetable garden.

Stores often sell small plastic watering containers with the sand toys, even at dollar stores. These are perfect for little hands to control. But if you don't have a small watering bucket, a pitcher, a hose with a controlled water flow, or even a squeezable sports or water bottle will work.

Your toddler will look forward to heading outdoors and helping Mommy. And she may surprise you and turn out to be a great little gardener! As well, your little one can see the fruits of her labor when the forget-me-nots flower or the summer squash sprout.

Skills learned

Knowledge of different types of vegetables or flowers will stem from your little one's helping with the upkeep of the garden. She also will learn colors, as both types of gardens are sure to produce brilliant hues. Your toddler will observe that things can grow from planting seeds as well as learn to differentiate between a weed and a flower or plant. Your child will see that when properly nurtured, living things grow and flourish. But perhaps most importantly, your little one will learn to appreciate and love God's wonderful creation.

Involve your toddler with raking leaves.

Aah. Autumn leaves. Crisp air. What a beautiful and refreshing time of year. Why not let your toddler enjoy it by getting him involved in raking leaves or scooping them into a bag? This task can be fun when you see how much your little boy loves handling the leaves. Your toddler can even get in a little play time while you rake another area.

Get your toddler a small plastic rake, or saw off the handle of an old rake, and watch your child's enthusiasm go sky high as he makes a little pile of leaves. Your little one will feel proud of the accomplishment. Even though the raking job won't be perfect, the time with your toddler will be.

Skills learned

Your child can learn more about nature—specifically types of trees and what their leaves look like—by getting involved in gathering leaves. You can show him that leaves become dry and brittle when they fall from trees. Your little one also can learn some of the vivid colors of nature—red, yellow, orange, green, and brown—and how beautiful God made the world.

Make bathing the dog a team effort.

The thought of trying to shampoo your dog while looking after a toddler may make you want to growl all the way to the groomer. But before you flee, try involving your toddler in the process. Get your little one excited about it, and turn it into your little project together. You can do your "project" at a set time each week. Your toddler may even look forward to the next time.

Give your toddler certain jobs such as squirting the soap on the wet pooch or blotting it with a towel after the soap is rinsed. Or maybe your child can play with the dog so it doesn't try to run away when you are washing it. Kids love pets, and this is a wonderful opportunity to help them begin to take responsibility.

Skills learned

Whether you just brought home a new puppy or your dog is older than your toddler, you can teach your little girl or boy a few new tricks when it comes to washing the dog. Your toddler can learn the process—wet, then wash with soap, then rinse—and that a dog needs a bath just like people do.

Have your toddler help out with the yard work.

Leaves are everywhere. Weeds are swallowing your plants. Your yard needs serious attention. But so does your toddler. Oh, what to do. One way to handle a situation like this—which probably arises frequently when you have a toddler—is to try to tend to both at the same time. You can do this by involving your toddler in what you need to accomplish. Granted, this won't work for every task, but, for many, a little creativity and thought is all you need.

When you have yard work piling up, for example, give your toddler a basket, bag, or sand bucket and have her collect pinecones, sticks, and pine needles that have fallen in the yard. Your little one will love helping out—toddlers like to do what grown-ups do, and the tension often comes from trying to keep them from doing so. In addition to keeping your toddler near you and occupied, this activity will help clear the lawn for mowing later. You may want to save the pinecones for craft activities at a later date.

Skills learned

Your toddler will learn responsibility in taking care of your lawn, and you can tell her how God wants us to take good care of all our things, which are his precious gifts. Your little one also will gain confidence and a sense of accomplishment as she was able to complete a task "all by myself!"

Let your toddler help you plant a vegetable garden.

Get out your toddler's sand shovels, or get a small (safe) shovel from your local home-improvement store if you're a serious gardener. He could put on a pair of old, thin gloves if you want to keep his nails clean. Put an old pair of jeans on him and a shirt you don't care about getting filthy and head out to the garden spot together.

Your little boy will enjoy watching and imitating you as you turn the dirt to prepare for the planting. When it comes time to plant, he can help dig the holes and bring you the potted plants. You may want to sort and line up the potted plants in the order you will want them handed to you. A little patience on your part is what will help nurture your little one's confidence in this activity.

You may be thinking, "Christopher is going to get so dirty!" True. But don't worry about it. After all, how long can it take to clean up? You're going to give your toddler a bath anyway—just do your gardening first, then plop your child in the tub. This may mean changing the planned order of things in your day and not taking a bath in the morning.

It will be well worth it to your toddler as he becomes Daddy's or Mommy's little helper.

Love is patient . . . it is not easily angered.

1 Corinthians 13:4–5

Skills learned

Doing this activity together will teach your toddler the different steps involved in planting a garden. He also will learn what a tomato plant looks like versus a pepper plant, then later what the harvest itself looks like.

Have your toddler brush your family's dog.

Give your toddler a large brush (now the designated dog brush) and briefly show her how to brush the dog. Tell your child to brush deep through the fur and to get all the places, even the dog's ears and tummy. Then let her take over. Meanwhile, hang some laundry, open the mail, pay some bills, or sweep the porch. For obvious reasons, brushing the dog is better done outside, if your dog won't run away. If that doesn't work, try doing it inside the dog's bed or in a spot on the patio. Probably once brushing begins, your dog will enjoy it and stay put. When your toddler is done, have her place the brush in a special spot for next time.

You may even choose to reward your child by paying her a small sum for doing this task each week.

Skills learned

Your toddler will learn about responsibility by taking on the task of brushing your dog. She will learn how to take care of a pet. Your child also will begin to learn about money—and putting it in a bank—if you choose to pay her for a job well done.

Let your toddler play with sand and funnels.

If you live near the beach, this is an easy one. If not, perhaps you can get your hands on some sand or, as an alternative, use salt. Put some of the material you are using into a sand pail or bowl. Get out a funnel or funnels and maybe a small strainer. Then take these items and your toddler outside. Let him experiment with pouring and sifting. You also may want to bring a plastic or paper cup to make it simpler for him to scoop some sand into a funnel or strainer. Then he can try to get the sand back into the cup from the small end of the funnel. To your toddler, it will be like playing in a mini sandbox. And what child doesn't like a sandbox?

While your toddler is playing, you can rake leaves, wash your windows, do some office paperwork, or pay your bills.

Skills learned

By pouring and sifting sand, your toddler will learn how to aim to get the sand in the cup, improving hand-eye coordination, while also learning about the qualities of sand—how the tiny grains of sand slip quickly through the holes of a strainer.

Let your toddler blow bubbles using a straw.

As an alternative to traditional bubble-blowing using a wand, pour some bubble stuff into a plastic bowl, give your toddler a straw—or two or three—and have your child put the straw into her mouth. Submerge the other end of the straw into the bubble stuff and blow.

This will create several bubbles, which your toddler will find interesting and amusing. You may have to show your toddler how to make bubbles, but then your independent little one will be anxious to grab the straw from you and play. Your toddler can experiment with the straws a little by bending a straw and blowing the bubbles through the angle or by using straws of different lengths or widths (if you have them).

Go outdoors, and you won't have to worry about a mess with this soap-and-water activity. And with your toddler content as can be, it will be like you waved a magic wand.

Skills learned

Your toddler will learn a whole new way to blow bubbles and may even remember to pass this idea along to her children down the road.

Set up a washtub for your toddler's babies or action figures.

When you have things you need to do outside but would rather not involve your little one, let your toddler wash her babies or action figures outside near you. Get a large, nonbreakable (plastic or metal) bowl, sand bucket or pan, an older washcloth or sponge, a towel, and your child's plastic babies or action figures. Add a squirt or two of dish soap and fill the bowl, pan, or bucket with water.

Have your toddler give her dolls or figures a bath. You may want to add a couple of small bath toys to make the process more fun. Then, have her dry off and dress the toys.

Skills learned

Your toddler will enjoy being around you and will learn how to tend to people by caring for his or her babies or figures, including washing, drying, and dressing.

Let your toddler paint the driveway or wooden fence with water.

Grab a large, cheap paintbrush (you could even get an inexpensive basting brush at the grocery store) and a bucket of water and take them and your toddler outside. While you are pulling weeds, trimming bushes, raking leaves, or accomplishing any other outdoor chore, let your little girl paint the driveway or a wooden fence with the water. Your toddler can paint any picture or design, and there will be no mess involved. She will enjoy seeing the shapes she paints. Don't forget to bring a towel—your toddler will not stay dry, guaranteed.

You could take this activity one step further and let your toddler use some washable paint. (Oh, what did our parents ever do without it!) You will, of course, have to hose and clean this up, however. Diluting the paint with water first will help ease the cleanup process.

During this activity, your toddler can paint anything, anywhere she likes. Your child will appreciate and enjoy the freedom.

Skills learned

Your toddler can develop her creativity and, at the same time, learn that water on these surfaces dries and becomes invisible.

Let your toddler finger paint with yogurt.

You will want to do this one outside. Whether it's your dirty windows or your garden that's starving for attention, you can accomplish the task with your toddler by your side. Get a few different colors of yogurt and simply open the containers and set out some finger-painting paper. (If you don't have any, a trash bag spread out will work—but make sure you keep an eye on your child to make sure he or she stays safe.)

Your toddler will have a ball painting rainbows, cars, flowers, smiley faces, or just scribbling with the yogurt. And you won't have to worry about your little girl getting the "paint" on her face or in her hair or about your boy putting something dangerous in his mouth.

When you're done with your tasks (or your child's attention is diverted), you may hose off your toddler's hands, wipe them with a washcloth, or just go inside and clean up. This would be a great opportunity to schedule bath time.

Skills learned

Your toddler can learn to draw new things by experimenting with yogurt finger painting.

Let your toddler wash his bike or kid car.

Next time you want to polish your motorcycle or the inside of your car, give your toddler his own little spray bottle filled with water, along with a rag, and wheel your child's bike or plastic car over by your car or motorcycle. Have your toddler polish his vehicle too. Your toddler will pay close attention to and imitate you.

For safety reasons, you don't want your child climbing in your car or too near your motorcycle. But your little one will enjoy working side-by-side with Mommy or Daddy. Meanwhile, both of you will get a task accomplished.

A little effort will go a long way toward keeping your toddler content. And you will cherish memories such as these for a long time down the road.

Only be careful, and watch yourselves closely so that you do not forget the things your eyes have seen or let them slip from your heart as long as you live. Teach them to your children and to their children after them.

Deuteronomy 4:9

Skills learned

Cleaning his bike or car will accelerate your child's willingness to help take care of his belongings.

Let your toddler play with whipped topping.

Before you begin this activity, go ahead and put a bathing suit on your toddler. You obviously will want to do this activity outdoors. Lay out a trash bag and either spray or scoop a bunch of whipped topping onto it.

Then let your toddler play with the whipped topping, making designs with it using his or her fingers, and just have fun getting messy. Meanwhile, you can wash your car or the windows on your house or accomplish some other outdoor task, perhaps even sitting outside working on a part-time job.

When you're done, if you have the hose out, turn it on your toddler. Or you can make it bath time. You're going to give your toddler a bath anyway—save it for now, and you won't have to take the time to do two. Note: Keep a wet towel handy in case the quick hands of a child make a quick mess that needs a quick cleanup.

Skills learned

When playing with whipped topping, your toddler will learn about soft textures as well as general creativity and expressiveness.

Let your toddler make rock people and animals.

For something different, grab a few rocks from your driveway or off the side of the road. You may want to bring your toddler along to pick out a few and put them in a sand bucket. Round rocks are nice for this activity, but any size or shape will work.

Then set the rocks out on a table along with some crayons and washable markers for your toddler. Encourage him to draw faces on the rocks, maybe making one of them a turtle, or just color on them. If he decorates his rock to be an animal or other living being, it can become his pet rock. You may want to use one of his creations as a paperweight later. This activity is not hard, and it will bring new life to your toddler's creativity.

Skills learned

Coloring on rocks will encourage your toddler to use his imagination.

Take your work outside or to different rooms of the house.

Variety is the spice of your curious toddler's life. So if you have work to do at home for your job, be as flexible as you can for the benefit of your little one. Try to take your work with you out to your backyard or to a park bench. Or take your work from the office to the living room, the playroom, your toddler's room, even the bathroom while your toddler is splashing in the tub. Print something out from your computer and take it with you if that will allow you more flexibility. Or simply use this time to brainstorm about new ideas related to your work.

If your toddler can move around and still be near you, she is more likely to be content. And this way, your toddler will have different toys to play with in different atmospheres. Changing things around a bit minimizes boredom for you; it will do the same for your children.

Skills learned

If you are flexible and accommodating with your toddler, that is exactly what she will pick up from you. And these are characteristics that will help your child not only now but throughout her life.

Have your toddler hit the pavement with some sidewalk chalk.

If you're the parent of a toddler, there's a good chance you have some chalk in your house. But if not, you could pick some up at the grocery store. Have your toddler bring it when you have things to do outdoors.

But instead of just handing it to your toddler, give him some ideas to make drawing with chalk more interesting. If you're washing your car, have your toddler draw a car; if you are tending to the lawn, have your little one draw a flower or a tree; if you are raking leaves, have him draw a leaf. If the picture is too hard to draw, your toddler can look at it and give it a try. Or you may draw the outline of the picture for your little boy to color or copy. Your child's chalk art will soon be the talk of the neighborhood.

Skills learned

After practicing, your toddler will start to be able to look at something and copy the image.

Have your toddler help sweep your porch.

Often your independent little girl will want to do whatever Mom or Dad is doing. Use this to your advantage because it won't last. If your porch—or inside your house, for that matter—needs to be swept, grab the broom and let your toddler help. If you have a large outdoor broom, use that and give your toddler the smaller, inside broom. Or a small brush and dustpan may satisfy your little one. You could even borrow a neighbor's broom so you and your toddler both have one.

Show your toddler how to use a dustpan, and if you have only one, you can use a paper plate in its place. She actually will enjoy helping out and being with you and will be easy to handle while you get this, or another, job done.

Tip

Toddlers love to imitate their parents. Yours will be happy to help you, but have patience. It may be a new learning experience for your little one, but in no time, she will be a pro.

Skills learned

By helping out with sweeping the porch or floors, your toddler will learn how to sweep and use a dustpan as well as responsibility and the importance of taking care of belongings. You also can begin to teach your little one good, helpful habits.

Let your toddler draw make-up faces.

This activity is better done outside to be sure your toddler doesn't get make-up on anything important, such as your carpet. Also, start by dressing your toddler in play clothes that you don't mind getting stained.

Then, if you have old lipsticks or eye liners that you have saved but don't want anymore, put them in a paper bag or plastic bowl and give them to your toddler to use to draw faces on herself. Make sure you have a hand-held mirror and wet washcloth ready so your little one can see her artwork, and you can wipe it off so she can start over.

Encourage your toddler to draw a cat face with whiskers, a lion with a mane, a bunny face with whiskers, or any other animal you can think of. You can demonstrate for your toddler on paper or on her face so she knows how to make different faces. Then this activity should be a roaring success at keeping your little one out of your hair for a while.

Skills learned

Your little bundle of joy will have a lot of fun learning about the features of different creatures by copying their faces.

Give your toddler holey paper cups and a pot of water to play with.

Get out a variety of paper cups and bowls, and punch or poke several holes in each of them at different heights. Fill a pot with water, grab your toddler, and bring the cups, bowls, and pot outside. You'll want to dress your toddler in her bathing suit or clothes you don't mind getting wet. Let your child play and experiment with the cups and bowls by filling them with water, then lifting them out of the pot and watching the water spurt out the holes. Make sure there's at least one hole close to the bottom of each cup so the water doesn't stop coming out of the cup until it's almost empty. Your little girl will find the concept of leaks fascinating as you get outdoor chores accomplished or bring your work outdoors.

Skills learned

By experimenting with holey cups and bowls, your toddler will learn about leaks as she watches the water spurt out each hole until the water level shrinks below it.

Part II

Ideas in Fifteen Minutes or Less

*Activities that require
no more than fifteen minutes
of preparation*

3

What's Inside

We often have more time in a day than we think. We may spend some time in front of the television at night to chill out after a busy day. While you are doing that, or during another break in your day, you can be cutting squares of construction paper or magazine pictures or doing just a small amount of preparation for activities to keep your little girl or boy occupied while you do jobs indoors the next day. This chapter provides many ideas for activities you can give your toddler that take fifteen minutes or less of preparation.

Show your toddler how to make mulch people.

If you have any mulch in your yard, your toddler can make people out of it. All you need is one or two pieces, but you could get several and make a family of mulch people. (If you don't have any mulch but your neighbor does, he or she probably won't mind donating a few pieces to the cause.)

You also will need some pieces of yarn. Cut about five pieces of yarn the same size—between two inches and six inches long—for each mulch person your toddler will make. The middle of these pieces of yarn will be glued (with washable liquid school glue) to the top of the mulch held vertically and will become the hair. Also get two small twigs that can be glued to each mulch person as arms. Then your toddler can draw a face on each piece of mulch using washable markers.

You can demonstrate for your toddler quickly how to make one mulch person so he or she knows what to do. When finished with the project, your toddler will enjoy playing with his or her little creation.

Skills learned

This craft will stretch your toddler's imagination while he or she learns an important life lesson—that sometimes some pretty cool things can be found in the most unexpected places.

Tip

Prepare craft activities for your child quickly—and don't worry about being exact or perfect. Your little one will love what you do for him or her.

Set up a little station with many different textures for your toddler to feel.

You can create the station on a small table, a TV tray, or even on a towel on the floor. If you know you have a lot to do one day, you can set out some items the night before after your little boy or girl has gone down for the evening. Just use items you have lying around the house. The key here is variety. Your toddler will find the differences interesting. Some ideas include cotton, sandpaper, fur, felt, a sponge, rocks, leaves, feathers, and swatches of material such as satin, corduroy, and flannel.

You may want to place each different item on its own paper plate or napkin. This display will separate the items for your toddler and help the station stand out, showing your child that this is something special to look at.

Skills learned

Toddlers will enjoy discovering how different things feel. You can tell them that the satin is smooth, the sandpaper is rough, and the cotton is soft. This just touches on the things your little one can learn by exploring textures.

Tip

Set up stations with different activities for your toddler in the four corners of your den or another room. This will be four times the fun for your little one.

Print out pictures of one of your toddler's favorite things from the Internet.

Sometime when you're not busy (or not *as* busy), you can search the Internet for something your little boy or girl loves. Whether it's zoo animals or butterflies or trucks, you likely will find pictures online. Print out several of them. If you have the time, you could cut out the pictures and even laminate them so they last.

Save them for a time when you're very busy, then pull them out, and your toddler will love his or her little gift. You can involve your toddler when you search for items on the computer, but you will want to print them out when your toddler is taking a nap or not paying attention. After all, you don't want to ruin the whole surprise. The elements of surprise and discovery are what will keep your little one interested.

Skills learned

Your toddler will learn a lot from this idea, including the fact that every creature has a variety of appearances. Take the many different colors of butterflies, for example, or the different looks of elephants. Your little one also can get early exposure to searching for something on the Internet.

Pack an activity kit that you take with you to appointments.

It happens to everyone. Your sitter falls through when you have to go to the doctor or another appointment. If this happens, or if you don't want to spend the time and money to get a sitter, pack an activity kit to keep your toddler occupied while at appointments.

Get a small, plastic case, preferably larger than a standard sheet of paper and with a handle, and fill it with a variety of arts and crafts supplies that your toddler enjoys. Some ideas include stickers, washable markers and crayons, construction paper, drawing paper, coloring books, tape, and rubber stamps. This is sure to keep creative minds content for an extended period of time while you're at the doctor's office, at the salon, or at a meeting. It makes waiting time fun for moms, too! Draw pictures and have your toddler guess what they are. Color a picture together. Ask your little one to make a picture for you. (This idea also works great at restaurants.)

Skills learned

There's no limit to the skills an activity kit can offer. Your toddler can practice coloring in the lines, make artwork, and learn new words and pictures.

Save large boxes and turn them into little houses for your toddler.

Little kids love to play with boxes. When you buy something that comes in a big box, instead of throwing it away, save it for a rainy day. You can even stash it in the attic or storage space if you wish to use it later. You can cut windows and a door in the box. Line up two or three boxes and make it a condo.

To add zest, place some kitchen supplies, a toy phone, and a pillow and blanket inside the boxes. You could set a smaller box nearby and turn it into a doghouse or shelter for another pet by putting stuffed animals inside with a plastic bowl and a blanket or towel. The fun your little girl or boy will have pretending with boxes is far from make believe.

Skills learned

Your toddler can gain a sense of dimension and proportion as well as what goes where in a home from stocking and playing in his or her own little home made from cardboard boxes.

Keep construction paper of all different shapes and sizes on hand.

Cut different shapes out of construction paper and save them for a time when you need to occupy your toddler. Cut circles, ovals, squares, rectangles, triangles, diamonds, and hearts out of many different colors. Cut sheets of paper in half or in quarters for different sizes. Variety is your friend when it comes to occupying your little one.

A good time to do this is while you are sitting out on your porch or patio or while you are watching television at night, maybe during commercials. An hour-long program can have up to fifteen minutes of commercials. Then when you need a little time to yourself, give the paper pieces to your toddler. He or she can play with the colorful shapes, which will be fun to look at, and perhaps glue or tape them onto a sheet of paper, cardboard, a paper plate, or poster board. You will have a happy toddler and a precious piece of artwork.

Skills learned

Your little one can learn colors and shapes as well as express his or her creativity by playing with pieces of construction paper.

Tip

When you are giving your toddler a craft to do independently, it is best to use washable glue, markers, and crayons . . . just in case.

Cut out pictures from magazines that your toddler can use to make a collage.

Before you toss out old magazines, cut out all kinds of interesting pictures from them. Then when you don't want to be disturbed, give the pictures, some tape or a glue stick, and paper, cardboard, or poster board to your toddler. Show him or her how to tack down the pictures and make a collage.

If you have several magazines from which to cut, you may want to do a theme, such as food, the beach, cars and trucks, dresses, or animals. If you collect an assortment, you could get more than one collage from a batch of magazines or catalogs. You could take it a step further and let your toddler pick out all the pictures that go with a particular theme. Making a collage can be a bunch of fun for your little one.

Skills learned

From making collages, your child can develop a love for art. Your toddler also can improve coordination skills (by lining up or overlapping the pictures and sticking them down) and learn how to group things that go together.

Tip

You may want to get some decorative paper, like that used for scrapbooking, or paper with a border to add pizzazz to collages.

Make homemade beanbags for your toddler to play with.

If you have some socks and some beans, you can make this toy. Get out a few socks and grab a bag of dry beans from the pantry. Put a generous portion of beans in each sock, tie a knot in the top of each sock so the beans are secure inside, and you have a beanbag. If you don't have dry beans, pick some up next time you're at the store—they are very inexpensive—or use dry rice or noodles instead. And you could tie the top of each sock closed using ribbon or yarn.

You can make big beanbags and small ones from your toddler's socks. If you don't want to use worn socks, buy cheap ones from a store.

Your toddler can play with the beanbags (they will be fun to hold and squeeze) or try tossing them into a cardboard box while standing behind a line (made from a towel or string). You also could tape sheets of construction paper together and have your toddler try to toss the beanbags onto the yellow squares, for example.

Skills learned

Your toddler will learn how to make beanbags if he or she watches you making them, practice his or her motor skills by tossing the beanbags, and learn different colors.

Let your toddler dress up in some of your things.

Get out your hats, old and new. Maybe you have some outdated jewelry in your jewelry box you can pull out as well. Scarves are a nice touch too. You and your spouse probably have a few out-of-style shirts that your little one can try on or an old work uniform or hat. Put anything you can think of that won't harm your child and that you don't want anymore in a box and let your toddler play dress up. It won't matter if the items are too big as long as your toddler isn't tripping over anything. Other dress-up ideas: big sister's dance outfit or old Halloween costumes.

If possible, enable your toddler to look in a full-length mirror while dressing up.

Any props—such as a stethoscope, the stock page in the newspaper, or some scrap pieces of wood—will add to the enjoyment your little one will have imitating your or your spouse's profession.

Meanwhile, you can get some computer or other work done in the house.

Note: You might want to have the camera on hand for this one! It's sure to be a Kodak moment.

Skills learned

By dressing up, your toddler can learn different aspects of certain types of outfits and can improve his or her skills of putting on clothing.

Show your toddler how to make a bug collection using nuts.

Get out whole nuts in their shells—a variety of types, if you have them. And take just a few minutes to prepare some items that your toddler can glue onto the shells to make a variety of bugs. Get out some wiggly eyes for crafts if you have them. Also, colored candy dots used in cake decorating work for eyes, as do peppercorns. Also, cut several small strips of felt (about an inch or inch-and-a-half long and narrow). Use a variety of colors, if you have them. If you don't have felt, you can use fabric from your sewing box or from your toddler's old clothing or pieces of yarn. These pieces of felt, fabric, or yarn can be glued on the shells as bug legs or stripes.

The candy dots can be glued on the shells as spots. Chocolate sprinkles also can be used as a neat alternative in designing bugs or beetle shells.

Your toddler also can make small creatures, such as mice. The felt strips can be glued on as tails; peppercorns can be used to make stubby tails.

If you have a few extra minutes, you can paint the nutshells before they're decorated. A red nut with peppercorns could become a ladybug, for example.

This should keep your toddler occupied for a while because there are endless possibilities for making a variety of bugs. He or she can play with them when the glue dries.

Making a bug collection, in a nutshell, will keep your toddler from being pesky while you are busy.

Skills learned

Your toddler can learn to express his or her creativity and improve fine motor skills by gluing small parts.

Get several paper dolls and articles of clothing from the Internet.

If you have a toddler who likes or may like paper dolls, go to a search engine and simply type in "paper dolls." A variety of printable dolls will be at your disposal within seconds. No creativity on your part is needed here. You can just print and cut them out one night while you are watching a television program. Don't show the paper dolls to your toddler until you need some time to accomplish something. Then take them out and let your toddler dress the dolls in various outfits.

You can print the dolls and the clothing on card stock or photo paper for more durability, but regular printer paper will work too. You may use different shades of paper when printing out the dolls to represent various ethnicities. Either way, your toddler will enjoy getting the paper dolls all dolled up.

Skills learned

Your toddler will enhance his or her motor skills by fastening and unfastening different outfits on the paper dolls. Your little one also will learn that God made people with different skin tones.

Tip

The key to a lot of activities that will keep your toddler occupied is planning ahead. Just a little thought or preparation the night before a busy day will go a long way when you need it to.

Make a felt board and felt items for your toddler to rearrange to make scenes.

Using a hot glue gun or liquid school glue, glue a whole piece of felt (or two together) onto a piece of cardboard. Then cut several items out of different colors of felt. (If you don't have felt, you can buy it for around twenty cents a sheet at a craft store.) You can make the items part of a theme. For example, cut out several sea creatures and shells and make all or part of the background color blue to represent the water.

Some suggestions include an octopus, a jellyfish, a crab, a shell, a seahorse, a turtle, a starfish, and a dolphin. Make the creatures come to life by gluing wiggly eyes on them, or you may have your toddler take this final step. Add a sandy area (with a square of tan felt), and you can cut out a sand pail, a shovel, and a palm tree as well.

Cut out items in a theme that interests your child, such as cars with a traffic light and road, or a zoo with some cages and a bear, a snake, an alligator, and a monkey. Since felt sticks to itself, your toddler will love rearranging the items and making different scenes.

Put all the felt items in a lunch bag, and this activity can be taken on the road for play in the car or at an appointment.

Try this, and for a while your toddler should cling to this new project—and not to you.

Skills learned

Playing with the felt board will teach your toddler about the items in the particular theme you have chosen. He or she may learn new words and discover what certain creatures look like and where they live.

Set up a tent or fort in your house.

Build it, and they will come. This seems to ring true for forts and most little kids. They will appreciate a tent set up in your den or living room because to them, it's a giant fort. Your toddler will love setting up the tent the way he or she likes and being a little interior decorator. Suggest bringing in pillows and a sleeping bag as well as coloring books, a flashlight, toys, even a snack and some water. Your little one also will love the privacy of his or her own little "home."

If you don't have a tent, or if yours does not fit inside your home, make a fort by draping blankets over chairs.

If your toddler is like most, this type of activity will keep your busy little one out of the doghouse—and in the fort—for some time.

Skills learned

Your toddler can learn how to set up the inside of a tent and practice basic house-keeping skills, such as making a bed, that he or she learned from Mom or Dad.

Have your toddler make a rainbow poster.

Start with a white poster board or some other large, white paper. Draw an arch, any size you wish your toddler to color, to be the outline of a rainbow. Section the arch into six. Then outline each section in a different color of the rainbow, going in order: red, orange, yellow, green, blue, and purple. Next, cut a circle out of yellow construction paper and some raindrops out of blue construction paper.

Have your toddler color each section of the rainbow in the color in which it is outlined. Then have him glue the sun and rain onto the poster board. For an added effect, have your toddler glue cotton balls onto the poster board as clouds.

When he is finished, you may want to trim the outside edges of the poster board to suit the finished product. If you love it, frame it and hang it in your home.

This is one picture that is sure to brighten any room in your house—the very nature of rainbows.

Skills learned

By creating a rainbow scene, your toddler will learn the colors in a rainbow and how rainbows happen—when the sun shines while it is raining. Your little one also will realize and appreciate how beautiful God's creation really is.

Have your toddler design a tiger, zebra, or other striped creature with yarn.

Draw the outline of a tiger, zebra, or other striped animal on a piece of construction paper for your toddler. If you have it, match the color of the paper with the animal's color. For example, use orange for a tiger. Then cut several pieces of yarn, in the appropriate colors if possible, for your toddler to glue onto the animal shape as stripes (black for a tiger, for example). Either a washable glue stick or liquid school glue will work. Your toddler can paint on the liquid glue if you squirt some out into a plastic or paper bowl and give her a fairly small paintbrush.

You may want to cut a picture of that animal out of a magazine or print one from the Internet for your toddler (and perhaps you) to see and copy. Don't fret if your drawing skills are not alive and well. Your toddler won't care if the shape isn't perfect.

Your toddler will jump at the chance to create animals with all their interesting features.

Skills learned

Your toddler will learn about new types of animals and the base and stripe color of each animal.

Make a homemade clipboard for drawing on the go.

If your child likes to draw or color, this interest can be encouraged anywhere you go with a clipboard to hold your toddler's paper in place and to keep his writing instrument from poking holes through the paper.

Regular clipboards may be a little too heavy for your toddler to hold onto with one hand while drawing with the other. And you may not have one handy. However, you can make one easily for little or no cost. Cut a piece of cardboard from a box or tear the back cover of a notebook off and use it as the board. Use a clothespin or two for the clip(s). Now you can tear a page out of a coloring book or get some white paper, and your toddler can clip it to the board. This new clipboard will be lightweight and easy for little hands to handle. You may want to make the cardboard a little bigger than the paper that typically will be clipped to it for times when your toddler colors past the edge of the page. You may also want to hot-glue the back part of the clothespin to the cardboard.

Take the clipboard in the car for your toddler to draw on from his car seat, take it to an appointment, or just let your child use it around the house. Any way, it should make drawing more fun.

Skills learned

Watching you create this project, your toddler will begin to think innovatively and outside the lines. Over time, activities such as this will help you see the entrepreneur in your little boy or girl emerge.

Show your toddler how to create mosaic art.

Sometime when you have a few minutes, maybe while you're watching television or sitting out on your back porch relaxing after a long day, tear or cut up some sheets of construction paper in a variety of colors into small squares and put them in a plastic container.

Then when you have to get something accomplished and need to keep your toddler occupied, give the squares of paper to your toddler, along with some whole sheets of construction or white paper and a washable glue stick. On the whole sheets of paper, draw a few basic outlines of things your toddler will recognize, such as flowers, a car, a turtle, or a house.

Show your toddler how to glue the squares of paper inside the shapes to make mosaic pictures. Then hand the supplies over to your little one to create pictures.

Since mosaic art is imperfect anyway, your toddler's will surely be picture perfect.

Skills learned

Your toddler will improve motor skills as he or she works on attaching the paper pieces while staying in the lines. Your child also will learn about a new form of artwork.

Show your toddler how to make a string of hearts for Valentine's Day.

Fold red, white, and pink paper and cut half hearts so that they unfold into symmetrical hearts. Try to make them similar in size—maybe two or three inches tall—but perfection is not necessary. Give your toddler a pile of hearts and a hole puncher and show her how to punch two holes in the top of each heart. Let your toddler punch all the holes, if it is not too difficult a task for her.

Then, using yarn or ribbon, show your child how to weave in one hole and out the other. Let your toddler continue until all the hearts are strung together. When the project is finished, don't forget to tie or tape both ends of the string to something in the house or drape it on your fridge with magnets, and you will have a lovely Valentine's Day decoration.

A cheerful heart is good medicine.

Proverbs 17:22

Skills learned

A major skill your little one can learn by weaving is hand-eye coordination. Also, when the project is displayed in your home, the confidence and pride your toddler learns to have in her abilities is sure to warm your heart.

Have your toddler make Christmas tree ornaments from poster board.

When you have a few minutes—at nap time, in the early morning, or in the evening, trace a paper or plastic cup several times on a poster board. Cut the circles out, and let your little one show his creativity by coloring or decorating them with arts and crafts supplies such as glitter glue, ribbon, or cotton.

Later, when you're not busy anymore, punch a hole close to the edge of each circle. Have your toddler slide a piece of yarn through each hole. Tie the yarn, and you have a homemade set of Christmas tree ornaments. Don't forget to jot the year on the backs.

For additional shapes, trace Christmas cookie cutters and cut the shapes out, have your toddler decorate them, punch a hole, and tie a yarn loop.

Older toddlers may be able to cut out the shapes well with safety scissors. If your toddler cuts them out, use construction paper instead of poster board to make cutting easier.

Skills learned

Your child will gain confidence by creating some of your Christmas decorations. He also will learn to cut on the lines and express creativity.

Have your toddler make "snow cones."

Grab a brown paper bag or basket for both you and your toddler. Go outside together and collect a bunch of pinecones of varying sizes.

Go back inside and get out a clump of cotton balls. Demonstrate how to make one "snow cone." Fluff the cotton by pulling it apart a bit, then stuff it into the crevices of the pinecone to create the appearance of snow.

Let your toddler do the rest while you accomplish what you need to do. You don't even need glue to create these lovely winter decorations that can be displayed throughout your home. You may want to display them in a basket or a bowl or line them up along a shelf. The finished product is simple, yet beautiful, and brings a touch of nature indoors.

Skills learned

Your toddler will learn about the contrasting textures of pinecones (prickly) and cotton (soft). He or she also will learn about the beauty found in the things of nature.

Have your toddler make a personalized memory game.

When you have a few extra minutes, perhaps while you are waiting at the doctor's office or watching television at night, cut some equal-sized squares of card stock or cut some index cards in half. Then when you need an activity to keep your toddler busy, give her two sheets of stickers that are the same and have her place one sticker on each card until the stickers are used up.

With two sheets of stickers, you are assured of at least two of each picture. An alternative to using stickers is to have your child glue unneeded copies of family photos on the cards. You don't need to have two of the same picture; you can include any two pictures of the same person or pet. Your toddler can attach the pictures to the cards using a washable glue stick.

A third option is to cut pairs of similar pictures out of magazines and glue them to the cards.

After the homemade memory game is finished, flip the cards over and take turns trying to find pictures that match. Your little girl's personal touch on the game is sure to make a lasting memory for you both.

Skills learned

Your toddler will strengthen memory skills, learn to glue pictures straight, and perhaps learn new words or pictures.

Show your toddler how to make a construction paper chain to be used as Christmas decor.

Cut thin strips of any combination of red, green, and white construction paper. Using a washable glue stick, show your toddler how to attach the two ends to make a loop. Make another loop through the first loop. Demonstrate making a few loops just before you need some time to get something done. Then have your toddler continue the chain in any colors he likes.

This project can go on for as long as your child is content. Your toddler can make short chains and long chains with big loops or smaller loops. Place no limits on your toddler; instead, let him express creativity. As with any craft, the more it is your child's project, the more you both will love it.

To round out your day, you can hang short chains or single loops from your Christmas tree or on doorknobs; longer chains may be draped as holiday garland in your toddler's room, play area, or anywhere you wish.

Skills learned

Your toddler will learn hand-eye coordination as well as see how chains come together by creating one out of construction paper.

Let your toddler make her own Valentine's Day cards.

Cut sheets of construction paper or card stock in half, then fold each remaining piece in half. In just a few minutes, you will have several cards. Also fold some paper in half and cut half a heart so that when you unfold it, it is symmetrical. Repeat to make several hearts of varying sizes. You also may want to get out some stickers and tissue paper torn into small pieces.

Show your toddler some different ideas for gluing hearts and tissue paper on the cards and sticking stickers. You also could cut heart pictures and X's and O's from magazines. Then hand over the supplies, along with a washable glue stick or washable liquid school glue, to your toddler and let her create the cards any way she sees fit.

Your child will love having the freedom to create the cards. Don't forget to look over occasionally and encourage her creativity and admire the magic those little hands have performed.

Later you may want to help your child write something on the cards and send them to Grandma, Grandpa, friends, or preschool classmates. You may even want to keep one or two cards and frame them.

If you don't have the supplies you want to make cards, spend a couple of dollars on craft supplies instead of on store-bought cards. The end product will be much sweeter.

Skills learned

Your child will learn confidence in her abilities, creativity, and the importance of giving the gift of love while feeling proud of her work of art.

Have your toddler make collages out of Christmas cards.

After Christmas, be sure to save all your Christmas cards. Then sometime when you have a few minutes, cut out all the pictures and some sayings.

When you have to get something accomplished, have your toddler glue the pictures on a piece of cardboard, poster board, or plain-colored card stock. You could even fold a few pieces of card stock in half and let your toddler express his creativity by making a card out of cards.

The cards your toddler creates can be sent to grandparents or friends next Christmas. The Christmas card collage idea can occupy your toddler after Christmas, or you can stash the cards away and let your toddler make collages before the following Christmas or at both times.

Date and save collages from year to year and see how they evolve. This idea also works great with birthday cards. Either way, you can't lose with this idea. Pictures on cards are beautiful and will make gorgeous collages any way they are arranged. They are sure to bring warmth to the chilly holiday season.

Skills learned

Designing collages will build upon your child's creativity and self-esteem as he shows off the finished product.

Tip

Keep a large shoebox, plastic bin, or gift bag for all cards you receive.

Have your toddler "dress" drawings of a boy and girl.

Cut small squares from an old pair of jeans and a couple of old shirts or dresses. You may want to use swatches from clothing that has a stain on it and won't be worn anymore. Then draw the outline of a boy and a girl on two sheets of computer paper, construction paper, card stock, or cardboard. Don't worry about your creative abilities. A simple outline will work great, and your toddler won't care about having a perfect drawing. But be sure to draw the outlines of shirts, pants, shorts, or dresses as well as accessories such as hats, a purse, or shoes, if you wish.

Make sure you cut the pieces of fabric small enough so your child can glue several on the outlines of the boy and girl. Give the drawings and the swatches of material, along with a washable glue stick, to your toddler. Have him glue the material onto the boy and girl shapes as clothing. Some denim pieces could be attached as jeans, for example.

The appeal of this activity could last longer than your toddler's jeans.

Skills learned

By dressing the paper people, your toddler will practice staying within the lines and learn about different fabric textures (cotton is soft, denim is rougher, corduroy has ridges) and how boys and girls dress differently.

Have your toddler make wrapping paper collages.

After your toddler's next birthday party, save a piece of wrapping paper from each gift. Later, you and your child can cut the paper into a few small pieces. Get part of a poster board or a fairly large piece of cardboard. Spread out the wrapping paper pieces on a paper plate and give them, the cardboard, and a washable glue stick to your toddler and have her make a wrapping paper collage.

Encourage your toddler to fill in all the blank spaces with paper. (Or you could glue a sheet of tissue paper onto the cardboard before your toddler glues on the wrapping paper. That way, any spaces not covered by wrapping paper will have some color.)

When your toddler finishes and the glue dries, write your child's name, the occasion, and the date on the back of the cardboard, along with the names of the people who attended the party or gave gifts. You will have a beautiful piece of artwork with your little one's touch. You may even want to have it framed and hung in your child's room or the playroom. Making a collage also can be a good activity at Christmastime or after any other occasion where gifts are received.

Skills learned

Making a wrapping paper collage will be a fun way for your toddler to express her creativity. And since it is sure to turn out beautifully, your toddler will be proud of the finished work of art. It is a sure way to build self-esteem.

127

Let your toddler decorate cupcakes.

After first making sure you have a can of frosting and some sprinkles on hand, mix up a box of cupcakes the night before you anticipate a busy day. A boxed mix takes just a few minutes to make. Make some regular and mini cupcakes, if you have the pans. Your toddler will appreciate the variety.

Do not frost or decorate the cupcakes. Just let them cool and cover them overnight.

The next day, show the cupcakes to your toddler. Get out the can of frosting, the sprinkles, and a plastic knife or a small spatula, and set your child at the table. Show or tell your toddler what to do, set out a plate on which to put the decorated cupcakes, and let your toddler frost and decorate them however he wants.

Your toddler will love the freedom that making his very own project offers—and, of course, will enjoy the after-dinner dessert.

You also may deliver some of the goodies to a friend with small children or a neighbor. Your toddler will enjoy showing off his decorating abilities to Daddy (or Mommy) when he or she gets home from work.

After your toddler is done creating, you simply will have to wipe the table and sweep the floor when you have a minute. This is a small price to pay for the time you will get to yourself and the joy the project will bring to your little one.

Patience is better than pride.

Ecclesiastes 7:8

Skills learned

Although you may not want to do this project often, once in a while this special treat will begin to teach your child part of the baking process—the fun part. In addition, your toddler will feel your trust as you give your little one decorating freedom. This project also will encourage creativity, and your child will feel proud of his accomplishment, which will be a treat to his self-esteem.

Show your toddler how to make crafts with fall leaves.

To prepare for this project, sometime when you and your toddler are outside during the fall or perhaps on the way in from the grocery store, pick up about a dozen fall leaves. Then inside, on a piece of construction paper, draw a simple tree trunk and some branches. (A ten-second sketch will do fine.) When you need some time to yourself, show your toddler how to break the dry leaves into small pieces on a paper plate. Your little one should enjoy crumpling the leaves because of their crunchy texture.

Then with liquid school glue, have him or her glue pieces of leaves on the branches and on the bottom of the picture, as though leaves had fallen from the tree to the ground. This is a simple way to get in touch with nature, and it is sure to leave a lasting memory with your child.

Skills learned

By creating a fall tree, your toddler can begin to learn about the season and how it is the time of year when trees begin to shed their leaves. He or she also can learn that God made the leaves in the trees to live, just like people.

Have your toddler make puppets.

Your toddler can make a variety of finger or hand puppets using her old gloves and socks, paper lunch bags, or even her own hand. Choose one type of puppet at a time, but let your toddler make a few puppets, then she will have them to play with or can put on a puppet show for stuffed animals, action figures, or dolls.

To make hand puppets, draw a face on your toddler's hand while it is in a fist to occupy her anywhere. For glove finger puppets, start the process yourself by cutting the fingers off the gloves. Small or large socks as well as lunch bags are ready to go.

Give your child some washable liquid school glue along with items to glue onto the puppets. These items may include wiggly eyes, yarn for arms and hair, and felt for mouths, tongues, ears, and noses.

Let your toddler use her imagination. As with any of your child's projects, don't worry about their not being perfect. Having something crafted by those little fingers will make it perfect in your mind. Plus, this craft will buy you some bonus time because after your toddler makes the puppets, she will take time to play with them.

Making puppets will help you keep control of your toddler while you get a much-needed project done.

Skills learned

By creating puppets from scratch, your toddler will learn how to make a puppet as well as improve her knowledge of parts of the face and body.

Have your toddler make a doorknob sign.

To start this project, cut a piece of cardboard sized to hang from a doorknob—maybe about four or five inches wide and any length. Cut the letters in your toddler's name out of a magazine. Also cut out a few pictures of things that interest your child.

Give your toddler the cardboard, letters, a washable glue stick, crayons, washable markers, and anything else he may use to decorate the sign. Have your toddler glue his name and pictures on the sign and color it. You may want to write his name on a piece of paper so he can copy it.

When the sign is finished, staple a piece of yarn onto both ends at the top and hang it from the door to your toddler's room.

This fun activity will open new doors to your child's creative thinking.

Skills learned

By making a doorknob sign, your toddler can learn the correct order of the letters in his name. Your toddler also will take pride and confidence in having a hand in decorating his room.

Make figures from interesting pictures on cardboard boxes.

As parents of toddlers, we all buy boxed items at the grocery store that feature pictures of the latest cartoon characters, cereal "mascots," or other popular icons. The second you walk into the grocery store, your toddler turns on her marketing radar, which with time often becomes simply too difficult to resist.

The images are everywhere—on cracker boxes, fruit snack boxes, yogurt cartons, and the list goes on. Whether it's Dora the Explorer Fruit Snacks or SpongeBob Cheese Nips, the marketers of these products have made the most of these images—now it's time for you to do the same. Since your toddler likes them, save them. Before you toss out the boxes, cut out the pictures and keep them in a shoebox.

In one of those rare moments when you have some time, make a straight cut at the bottom of each image, then make each image stand up one of two ways. You could cut a small, rectangular-shaped piece of cardboard with a straight-edged bottom and tape it to the back of each image, giving it a picture-frame stand. Or, you could cut an approximately half-inch slit in the bottom of each image; then cut another slit in a small, rectangular-shaped piece of cardboard; and fit the two slits together.

Pull the images out for your toddler to play with when you need some time without interruptions. She can set up all the images and let her imagination run wild.

Skills learned

Your child will stretch her imagination playing with several cardboard box figures. Your toddler also may learn to look for fun in unique places and things.

Mix up some homemade play dough for your toddler.

The night before a busy day, take a few minutes and make some home-made play dough your toddler can play with the next day. It's nontoxic and easy and inexpensive to make, and chances are you already have the ingredients you need in your pantry. You and your little boy can mix it up together, then your child will have something to look forward to the next day.

Let your toddler play with it at the table, at a plastic kid's table, or on some cardboard on a noncarpeted floor. Give your toddler some cookie cutters to cut shapes in the dough.

Here's how to make it:

Mix 1 cup cold water with 1 cup salt, 2 teaspoons vegetable oil, and food coloring. Gradually add a mixture of 3 cups flour and 2 tablespoons of cornstarch until the mixture reaches the bread-dough consistency. That's all there is to it. Within a few minutes, you'll have a new activity that will help mold your child's character.

Skills learned

This activity can teach your toddler the basics of making play dough; the textures of different ingredients such as flour, salt, and cornstarch; perhaps even new shapes from the cookie cutters. Your toddler also will improve his fine motor skills by molding the dough into different shapes and objects.

Have your toddler glue dried flower petals.

When your spouse gives you roses, don't toss them out when they begin to wilt. Instead, tie the stems together and hang them upside down to dry.

After a day or two, they'll be dry. Then pluck the petals (your toddler can help) and put them in a nonbreakable bowl. Give your toddler some washable liquid school glue and some construction paper and let her create a work of art with the dried petals. Petals from other types of flowers may work as well, if they are big enough for your child to handle.

The uniqueness of this art project will pique your toddler's interest, and any arrangement she makes is sure to be a beautiful creation.

Skills learned

By making art with flower petals, your toddler's knowledge about nature will blossom. She will learn about different types of flowers, the kinds of petals they have, and their colors.

Show your toddler how to make flowers and trees using wooden craft sticks.

While you're perched in front of the television one night, grab four sheets of construction paper—one each of green, red, white, and any other color. From the green paper, cut two scallop-edged ovals about four inches long to resemble a treetop. From the red, cut some small circles to represent apples to go on the trees. From the extra color, cut some flower petals a couple of inches long. Cut enough to make two flowers. From the white paper, cut two circles about an inch in diameter. These will be the centers of the flowers.

When you are ready for your toddler to make the trees and flowers, show him how to glue the parts together on the sticks. Glue the green treetops to wooden craft sticks, then glue the apples on the treetops. For flowers, glue petals on wooden craft sticks, then glue a white circle at the center of each flower.

Just get your toddler started, then let him do the rest. If you can without breaking concentration on your task at hand, talk to your little one during this activity and explain how God made flowers and trees.

Skills learned

By making these replicas of nature, your child will learn that God created these things and that apples grow on trees and flowers come in all shapes and colors.

Let your toddler be her own one-person band.

If you can concentrate on your jobs with some background noise, this activity will sound appealing to your toddler. Turn on some music and fetch some "instruments" with which your little girl can play along. Some ideas:

- A wooden spoon or a hairbrush can make a good microphone.
- Grab some chopsticks to be used as drumsticks and a small box or plastic storage container for a drum. (This container can be used to store the instruments and cart them to a convenient room. Make sure your little one is careful with the chopsticks.)
- If your little one has a children's play piano or keyboard, pull it out too.
- Put some dry beans from your pantry into a plastic Easter egg or two to make maracas. (You may want to tape the edges shut.)
- You also can get some sleigh bells out of your Christmas items.
- And, for the brave, what toddler hasn't already learned that pot lids make great cymbals?

Put all your chosen instruments in a location convenient for you while you accomplish your work, and it will create a harmonious environment for your toddler.

Skills learned

Your little one will learn how many different "instruments," or everyday items, make sound, and she will learn to distinguish high pitches from low pitches.

Tip

A harmonica would not be a recommended instrument to include in this mix.

Show your precious one how to make a snowman out of plastic foam balls.

Next time you are near a craft store, stop and pick up three or six plastic foam balls—in three different but close sizes, if possible. Stick them in a closet and pull them out at a time (in the winter) when you need to keep your little one occupied. Your toddler then can use them to make a snowman.

You can prepare the parts for the snowman in just a few minutes' time by following these suggestions:

- Slice a cap off of the largest plastic foam ball with a knife. This ball will serve as the base of the snowman.
- Glue the three balls together.
- Slice a narrow strip off a carrot and cut it about an inch or so long. This can be stuck into the face as the nose.
- Peppercorns can be pushed into the plastic foam as eyes.
- Use peppercorns or redhots to make a line for the mouth. Glue if necessary.
- Push or glue three or four silver-colored cake decorating beads or peppercorns into the plastic foam as buttons on the middle section.
- Get two sticks to poke into the snowman's body as arms.
- Have your toddler set a medicine cup painted black the day before on top of the snowman for the hat.

To enable your toddler to do this activity independently, draw a sketch of the snowman for him to copy, or you could make one of your own ahead of time. Your precious one will have a ball, and this wintry craft will bring warmth to your home.

Skills learned

By making a snowman using plastic foam, your toddler will learn how to make a real one outside. He also will learn about the texture and versatility of plastic foam and improve fine motor skills by putting all the pieces of the snowman together.

Have your toddler set the table using paper or plastic.

Paper or plastic? Let your toddler decide. Once in a while on a busy day, have something more casual for dinner such as hamburgers, hot dogs, sandwiches, or salads and have your toddler set the table with nonbreakable dinnerware.

Get out paper or plastic plates and cups, plastic utensils if you have them, and some napkins. Count out just enough for your family.

Then have your toddler put one set out for each person (spread around the table until the items are used up). She may even be able to fill the cups with water from the spout on the refrigerator or using a light-weight plastic pitcher not filled too full.

Your little one will love to help out by doing a grown-up task. And besides occupying your toddler for a little while, you will save time later by not having as many dishes to wash. This is a win-win activity that will serve you well on a busy day.

Skills learned

By setting the table, your toddler will learn about jobs and responsibilities. Also, your pride and joy will feel good about herself after finishing the job and looking back at the dinner table she set "all by myself."

Have your toddler design a decorative kite.

Cut a large (ten to twelve inches long) diamond out of white paper, card stock, or cardboard. Then tear up small pieces of tissue paper—any number of colors will be beautiful. Have your toddler cover the diamond shape with liquid washable school glue and the tissue paper. Have him be generous with the glue and the tissue paper, even overlapping or layering the paper.

Then punch a hole in one corner, thread some string or ribbon through the hole, and tie a knot. The kite can be fastened around a ceiling fan chain, a doorknob, or a nail on the wall in your toddler's room for him to enjoy. Since the kite will be fun to make and fun to look at, this is one idea that will really fly with your toddler.

Skills learned

Your young toddler can master his colors by creating a kite with multiple colors of tissue paper. He also can learn to recognize a diamond shape and how kites work—that people fly them by holding onto a string attached to the kite.

Show your toddler how to make her own book.

Prepare for this activity by cutting a few sheets of construction paper or card stock in quarters. Then punch about four holes near the top of all the sheets, making sure the holes line up. These will be the pages in the book. To design the pages, give your toddler several pictures cut out of magazines or printed from the Internet, along with some stickers, and have her glue them onto the pages using a washable glue stick. Go a step further and have all the pictures be in a particular theme, such as animals, food, or people.

Set out some crayons or washable markers for your toddler as well, in case she wants to draw or color any pages.

When your child is finished creating the pages of her book, tie it together by threading one piece of yarn through the first hole of each page and tying it, then repeating the process for each of the four holes.

Skills learned

Your toddler can learn how a book is created—page by page. She also can associate what things go together by "writing" a book with a theme.

Have your toddler decorate bookmarks as gifts.

Cut one or more rectangles the size of a bookmark from card stock or cardboard. Give your toddler a washable glue stick and a variety of craft supplies with which to decorate the bookmarks. Some craft supply suggestions include cut pieces of raffia, tissue paper, wrapping paper, streamers, construction paper, magazine pictures, pictures of something your toddler likes printed from the Internet, photographs, foam craft shapes, fabric squares, sequins, and pictures cut from greeting cards. Your toddler may want to make two or three bookmarks because they are small. So be ready with enough supplies on hand so you can take advantage of the time you can get.

You can punch holes every inch or so around the outside border of each bookmark and have your toddler weave thin ribbon or yarn through the holes. (You can tie the knot and clip the yarn or ribbon when your child is done weaving.)

This project will be lots of fun. You and your toddler can use the finished bookmarks, or you both can give them away as gifts.

Skills learned

Your toddler will be able to express his or her creativity while learning to weave, improving fine motor skills, and gaining self-confidence as he or she sees you using and loving your bookmark. This project also will encourage reading and maybe even giving as your toddler sees how happy the gift makes someone.

Have your toddler design picture frames.

Take a moment when you can and pre-cut a frame or two out of cardboard. Start by cutting a rectangle, then cut another rectangle inside. You may want to make the opening three inches by five inches or four inches by six inches—standard photo sizes. But it is not necessary to measure it; you can always crop a photo later to fit in the frame.

When making the first cut, be sure to make it big enough so that you can leave a couple of inches around the frame window for your toddler to decorate. This may sound complex, but it is quick and easy. You can make it even easier by starting with a greeting card. You also may make the frame from craft foam.

When you have prepared your frames, give your toddler whatever craft supplies you want—such as foam craft shapes, noodles, yarn, rickrack, scraps of wrapping paper or fabric, stickers, or small shells—and, using washable glue, have him attach the decorations.

When the frame is finished, you may tape a photo to the back, then glue on a magnet for the refrigerator or a square cardboard stand. You also may punch two holes in the top, tie a piece of yarn to the holes, and hang it on the wall.

These frames will go nicely in your toddler's room and make great gifts for grandparents. The frame will be as pretty as the picture.

Skills learned

Frame-making will boost your toddler's self-esteem as he makes something for the purpose of being displayed for all to see.

Cut out shapes of God's creation for your little one to decorate.

From a poster board or card stock, cut out a couple of shapes of God's creation that your toddler will enjoy decorating such as a butterfly, a bee, a turtle, a tree, a sun, a snake, a fish, or a flower.

To hold your child's interest the maximum amount of time, use items she really likes—maybe it's a whale or a starfish or a bunny. Just make simple cutouts—don't worry about perfection; your toddler won't.

Then tear up several small pieces of tissue paper in colors appropriate for the items cut out. Have your toddler glue the tissue paper onto the cutouts.

You also can show your toddler how to crumple up the tissue paper, then glue it down. This creates a 3-D effect that your toddler will find captivating. Your toddler will naturally have fun creating what God already created.

Bring them [your children] up in the training and instruction of the Lord.

Ephesians 6:4

Skills learned

Your toddler will learn about God's creation. You can teach her that the things she decorated all came from him, just like she did. Your child also will learn about textures—smooth versus crumpled tissue paper—and dimensions—2-D (flat) versus 3-D (crumpled).

Have your toddler glue seeds on drawings of appropriate fruits.

When you eat various fruits, save and dry the seeds. Some fruits whose seeds you may save include watermelon, orange, apple, pumpkin, and lemon.

When they are dry, put them in plastic cups, label them, and save them for a busy day. Then give them to your toddler—the seeds of one fruit at a time—along with the shape of the particular fruit they have come from cut out of construction paper of the appropriate color. For example, cut the shape of a slice of watermelon from red construction paper and give your child the watermelon seeds, then give him the orange seeds and a circle from orange construction paper, and so on.

Also give your toddler some washable liquid glue and have him stick the seeds on the fruit. By giving them to your child one fruit at a time, he won't mix them all up. If you have seeds from several fruits, you may have to split the activity into two separate occasions, depending on your toddler's attention span. The seeds will be fun for little fingers to handle as you plant deep-rooted memories for your pride and joy.

Then God said, "Let the land produce vegetation: seed-bearing plants and trees on the land that bear fruit with seed in it, according to their various kinds." And it was so.

Genesis 1:11

Skills learned

Gluing seeds on fruits will teach your child that all fruits have seeds, and he will learn to identify the different seeds.

Have your toddler design Easter cards.

Decorating Easter eggs is a project your children look forward to when the holiday rolls around each year. So why not extend the fun in a way that is less messy and that will keep your toddler busy for a bit?

Help your child get started with this project by making the card. Fold a sheet of construction paper in half and cut an egg shape out of the paper, leaving the fold in the card.

Give your toddler some crayons or washable markers and have her "color" the Easter egg shapes. Also cut some strips of wavy rickrack that your child can glue on the egg cards. If you don't have rickrack handy, you also may cut some pieces of construction paper with decorative scrapbooking scissors. Repeat for as many cards as your toddler is interested in making.

These cards can be mailed to grandparents or other relatives or given to Daddy or Mommy. Your toddler, who no doubt loves coloring Easter eggs, will enjoy the opportunity to color more (on the cards) without any help and where anything goes.

> Jesus said to her, "I am the resurrection and the life. He who believes in me will live, even though he dies; and whoever lives and believes in me will never die."
>
> John 11:25–26

Tip

Save any unused paper cutouts or other craft items in a box for future use by your toddler or for donation to her preschool or Sunday school.

Skills learned

Designing Easter egg cards will nurture your child's creativity as she improves coloring and fine motor skills. Your child also will feel a sense of accomplishment and ability from creating the project alone.

Make your toddler some sponge building blocks.

If you have some unused sponges in the house, you can cut them into squares and rectangles and make a set of soft "blocks" for your toddler to play with. You can cut them with a pair of scissors. The more sponges, the better for this activity, as it gives your toddler more to play with. Look for sponges at the dollar store next time you are there or pick some more up at the grocery store. Sponges make good building blocks because they come in a variety of bright colors, are lightweight and therefore more portable, and are soft and fun to touch and hold.

Keep the sponge blocks in a tote bag or backpack, and your toddler can take them along and play with them in the car.

Skills learned

Your toddler is like a sponge, ready to absorb anything in his or her environment, including the texture and weight of sponges as well as building and balancing skills.

Tip

Get ready to get to work right away when your toddler begins a new activity. That way, you maximize your time without too many interruptions.

Have your toddler match pictures of animal parts to the correct animals.

Start this activity for your little one by cutting several pictures of animals or other living beings out of magazines. (Make sure you save any free samples of children's nature and animal magazines you receive in the mail.) Then snip off the tiger's tail, the bird's beak, and the whale's tail.

Give all the magazine cutouts, a couple of pieces of construction paper, and a washable glue stick to your toddler. Have him glue the animal bodies on the paper, then glue on the matching tail or other part.

If you are really ambitious, you can laminate all the animals and their parts and glue a magnet on the back of each piece, and your toddler can play with them on the refrigerator while you are working in the kitchen.

The quality photography in magazines that are competing for your little one's attention will make this activity a roaring success.

Tip

When grandparents are looking for birthday and Christmas gift ideas for your little one, suggest a subscription to a children's educational, nature, or animal magazine. This will give your toddler plenty of magazines to cut pictures from on a regular basis.

Skills learned

By matching animals to their parts, your toddler will learn about many different types of animals and what they look like.

Have your toddler create people from magazine cutouts.

From old magazines or junk mail such as catalogs or brochures, cut out many different faces, bodies, and articles of clothing. Give your toddler all the pictures, a washable glue stick, and some construction paper, computer paper, cardboard, or whatever paper you have lying around the house. (Try to have the right number of body parts to make whole people. In other words, don't have an extra pair of shoes or a leftover head.)

Have your toddler glue together people on the paper. Show your child that she can use any face with any body with any hat with any shoes. Give your toddler total freedom to create any person she wants. This will be a fun, silly activity that will knock the socks off your toddler.

Skills learned

Making different people from magazine pictures will teach your toddler that just as she is creating unique people, God has created all of us as unique people, and he loves each person's individuality.

Tip
In a large box, begin saving every magazine, catalog, and brochure that contains anything that your toddler may find interesting. They will come in handy on many occasions.

Have your toddler make a set of flash cards with magazine pictures.

First cut some small, interesting pictures out of magazines. Make sure the pictures are on a level that your toddler will be able to understand, but also choose ones that will challenge your toddler when he is asked to identify them later. It would be a good idea to include pictures of things your little boy doesn't already know. Also, throw in a few things he does know well to encourage him later.

After you have selected and cut out the pictures (any number you want, maybe ten or twenty to start with), either use index cards, colored if you have them, or cut several squares of construction paper or colored card stock about that size.

When you're ready to get some work done, give the cards and the pictures to your toddler, and have him glue one picture on each card. (Give your child the same number of cards as pictures so it is not confusing to him.)

Later, when you can make some free time, you can hold up the pictures and tell your toddler what each one is, and see how soon he can guess each picture. You might print the word you are teaching under each picture.

Your toddler will find these flash cards fun to make and fun to use with Mom or Dad later.

Skills learned

These flash cards will teach your toddler new words, new pictures, and maybe even to begin identifying printed words.

Tip

Perhaps your toddler's pediatrician or your auto mechanic or hair dresser will be willing to donate old magazines to your collection for future activities rather than tossing them out.

Make a homemade puzzle for your toddler to piece together.

Picture this: Your toddler is putting together a puzzle that is a picture of your family, himself or herself, or a favorite animal. By making your own puzzle, you (or your toddler) can select the picture you want to use. Try to pick something your toddler has a special interest in. Get a picture from an old paperback book cover, a magazine cover or page, a photograph—perhaps enlarged—even a poster.

For added durability, glue the picture to cardboard first. Then cut your own puzzle pieces. Put the puzzle pieces in a shoebox or plastic container for a day when you need to keep your toddler busy. Then have him or her try to piece the puzzle together.

Your little one will be delighted to see the picture when it's finished. Add to the excitement and anticipation of the activity by not giving away the secret picture on the puzzle.

A homemade puzzle, which can be prepared relatively quickly when you have a few minutes to spare, will fit nicely into your busy day.

Skills learned

Building puzzles will strengthen your child's ability to solve problems and help him or her develop patience when figuring things out.

Have your toddler make dolls from panty hose.

Start this activity by putting one knee-high stocking inside the other in the pair to double the doll's durability. Give the knee-high stockings and a bunch of cotton balls (pulled apart a little) to your toddler. Have her stuff cotton gently into the stocking until it's fairly full. When this is done, tie a piece of ribbon or yarn around the end of the stocking. Tie another piece about five inches from the toe area. This section becomes the doll's head. You may want to make the ribbon long enough to tie a bow. A plaid Christmas ribbon would be cute.

Then you can hand the doll back to your toddler and also give her some washable liquid school glue, several cut pieces of yarn that your child can glue to the head for hair or a mustache, some sequins or mini pom-poms or pieces of felt that can be glued on as eyes and a nose, and a shorter piece of yarn that can be glued in an arch as a smile. You may choose to sew buttons down the middle of the doll for your toddler later.

Your little one will enjoy bringing some materials lying around the house to life and playing with the new doll.

Skills learned

Your toddler can learn how to put materials together to make a toy while learning to think creatively and look for fun in simple, everyday items.

Have your child make your Thanksgiving dinner place cards.

Pre-cut several small pictures out of magazines of things a person could be thankful for. Then cut several small, equally sized squares of card stock (maybe about four inches). Cut one card for each person that will be at your Thanksgiving dinner.

Give your toddler a washable glue stick, and ask her to select several pictures of things she is thankful for such as food, family, and pets, then glue them on the cards. When she is finished, you can write each person's name on a card. Or you may want to print out the guests' names from your computer, cut them apart, and have your toddler glue one on each card. Just wait to give your child the names until after she is finished with the pictures so she doesn't cover up the names with pictures.

You can have your toddler do this activity while you are preparing Thanksgiving dinner or on another day—whenever it will be most helpful to you.

If you are having dinner somewhere else, maybe at your parents' house, ask if they mind if their little granddaughter makes the place cards. Anyone will find them to be a special ingredient in your Thanksgiving meal.

Skills learned

This activity will help your toddler think about and realize what she is thankful for while also learning a bit about entertaining (by setting out place cards).

Show your toddler how to make clothespin art.

There are a lot of possibilities for decorated clothespins, which later can be clipped in a variety of places for display or put to good use.

Cut shapes of butterfly wings from sheets of construction paper, card stock, or craft foam. Your toddler can glue these on the tops of clothespins, then glue on wiggly eyes or tiny pieces of felt for eyes. Small pieces of yarn can be glued onto the paper or foam for butterfly designs. Cut green construction paper, which can be glued on the clothespins to make treetops. You also can cut flower petals, leaves for clothespin "branches," or wings to make a dragonfly. Cut eight pieces of yarn to be glued to the clothespin to make it a spider.

Once you have cut the paper or foam shapes and accessories you and your toddler want, give them, along with a washable glue stick, to your toddler. Briefly show him how to do the project, then set your child's imagination free.

The finished clothespins can be used to close bags of your toddler's favorite snacks or cereals, clipped onto ceiling fan chains for decoration, used to clip papers in your office or your toddler's art papers, used as refrigerator magnet clips, or put on homemade clipboards (see idea 98 on making clipboards). To use them as magnets, just cut a piece of magnet and glue it onto the back of the clothespin. You can never have too many clips. These crafts make great gifts, too.

Skills learned

Your toddler will learn about the different parts of whatever objects he creates and will feel proud of his accomplishment.

Send your toddler on a mini scavenger hunt throughout the house.

Start by tearing some sheets of construction paper into fairly small squares. Then after your toddler goes to bed one night, make a trail throughout the house using the pieces of paper. Have stops here and there. Lead the trail directly to some of your toddler's favorite toys that you have strategically placed throughout the house.

Have your toddler pick up each toy that the trail leads to and put it in a basket or bucket. Put a special treat for your toddler at the end, the final stop. You can tell your child that when she gets to something new, she will be all done with the game. Some suggestions for treats: a small toy, a coloring book, a new ball, or even a decorative pencil.

Be ready to get to work the minute your toddler starts the hunt so you can maximize your time. Your toddler surely will find a scavenger hunt fascinating, and you'll buy some more time at the end when she plays with the treat.

Skills learned

By participating in a mini scavenger hunt, your child will learn how to follow instructions—and that it pays to do so.

Have your toddler decorate small boxes to be used for gift-giving.

You may want to start by covering a shoebox or other small cardboard box in a paper bag or white printer paper when you can spare a few minutes, perhaps during your toddler's nap time. Or you may get small, white cardboard boxes from a craft store that are made for decorating. To keep your toddler occupied, give the box, a variety of craft supplies, and a washable glue stick to your toddler and have him decorate the box. Your little one will enjoy using little pieces of tissue paper, scraps of pretty wrapping paper, magazine pictures, streamer paper, foam craft shapes, photographs, or anything else you have lying around the house that can be glued to the box. Your toddler also may want to decorate using crayons or washable markers.

Later, toss some tissue paper inside the box, and your toddler can use it as a gift box for a friend's birthday, Mother's Day, Father's Day, or any occasion. These boxes will save you time later by not having to wrap a gift and will become keepsakes for the gift recipients.

Skills learned

Your child will learn to express himself creatively while learning to make giving special and personal.

Set up snack time for your toddler's dolls, stuffed animals, or action figures.

When your toddler is in bed one night, set out some dolls, stuffed animals, or action figures at a kid's table or use a box covered with a pillowcase or a towel for a table. If you have kid's chairs, set the toys on them. Set out a few place settings using appetizer or dessert-sized paper plates, some plastic spoons, decorative napkins, and small, five-ounce paper cups. Small unused plastic medicine cups work too.

Your toddler will be pleasantly surprised to see the set-up in the morning. It probably will make her want to play right away—so be prepared to get right to work on your jobs. First, set out some Cheerios, crackers, or any other snack that won't create a big mess. Put them in a plastic bowl with a spoon or ice cream scoop so your little one can dish them up for her friends. You may want to set out some water or milk too. This activity will be a treat for your little girl.

Skills learned

While your toddler is enjoying snack time with her pretend friends, she will improve motor skills and balance by scooping up the treats and putting them on the plates as well as by getting some Cheerios on a small plastic spoon to pretend to feed the dolls, stuffed animals, or figures. Your toddler will learn to get better at not spilling things.

Make simple stencils from which your toddler can create pictures.

A stencil is easy to make—just draw a picture on a piece of cardboard and cut the picture out from the middle (without cutting any other part of the cardboard). You don't have to draw the picture freehand. Other suggestions include tracing cookie cutters or cutting a small picture out of a coloring book, snack box, cereal box, or other material and drawing an outline around the picture onto the cardboard.

Then give your toddler some paper and crayons or colored pencils and show him how to reproduce the shape by drawing around the inside of it. Elaborate pictures are not necessary for your little one; small, simple pictures that your toddler can practice over and over are great.

Ideas for shapes include a star, a cloud, a flower, a spider, a snake, a lizard, a car, a butterfly, even just an assortment of geometric shapes for young toddlers. If making pictures, try to use ones your toddler especially likes. Introducing something new to your child through a stencil also is a neat idea.

Drawing from stencils should keep your mischievous toddler in line for a time while you chomp at the bit.

Tip

Even when you are very busy, take breaks, if only for ten minutes at a time, to focus on your precious little angel. Swing, go for a walk, read a book, or play a game. If you don't, these special days that you are blessed enough to be able to spend with your toddler will fly by right before your eyes.

Skills learned

Your little one will learn how to move his little fingers and hands to follow the lines of the stencils. He also can learn new shapes or pictures.

Decorate a shoebox in which your toddler can carry special toys when on the go.

Get a shoebox you don't need and cover it with wrapping paper that your toddler will find interesting—perhaps printed with her favorite characters or things she likes such as hearts or cars. You may want to pick some up next time you are at the store. This can become an on-the-go storage box for some of your toddler's favorite toys. Throw a baby blanket, bottle, and doll in the box, and it becomes your daughter's bed for her babies. Put some blocks, a piece of sandpaper, and a toy hammer and screwdriver in the box, and it can be your son's play toolbox. This interesting container will make your toddler see typical toys in a whole new light. You also could match the wrapping paper to the theme of the toys that your toddler will put in the box.

These boxes will hold not only your toddler's toys but also your little one's attention, whether at home, in the car, or at an appointment or meeting.

Skills learned

Your little girl will learn to use her imagination and think out of the box when choosing different items to play with in her new toy box.

Have your toddler make straw jewelry.

Buy a pack of straws at the grocery store or your local dollar store, if you don't already have some. Get the most colorful ones you can. Cut them into approximately one-inch pieces. Then give the straw pieces, placed in a nonbreakable bowl, and some pieces of yarn to your toddler. Have her string the straw pieces to make a necklace. Help your toddler tie the ends together on the finished product. You also can cut smaller pieces of straw—about a half-inch in size—and have your toddler string them to make bracelets or key chain decorations. (You'll want to keep keys on your regular key ring and attach this craft as decoration only, as the yarn may not be strong enough to hold the weight of the keys.)

These projects can be kept or given away as gifts from your precious little one. Your toddler will have so much fun with this activity that she will wear out the jewelry—not you.

Skills learned

Your child will improve her fine motor skills by stringing the pieces of straw. In addition, your toddler will feel confidence after being able to do the project independently.

Blow up several balloons for your toddler to bat around.

On a day when you have more to do than the time allotted, release some steam by blowing up five, ten, even fifteen balloons when you don't want to be disturbed. The more balloons, the more your toddler will be amazed. Your little one will love batting them around and kicking them.

Challenge your toddler to try to keep a balloon from touching the ground. This activity would work well if you have an open den or playroom area. Tie a ribbon to a couple of the balloons for something different. You even could draw funny faces on a few of them. You won't believe the fun your toddler can have with a 99-cent bag of balloons.

Note: Keep an eye on your little one to make sure that she doesn't put balloon pieces in her mouth. If a balloon pops, pick up the pieces right away for safety.

Skills learned

Your toddler will learn different colors and how balloons pop as well as enhance her coordination by trying to keep a balloon in the air.

Get out older toys for your toddler to rediscover.

Before you give away your toddler's old toys that you may have packed away, take them out one day and let your toddler explore them all over again. Your little one probably knows a lot more now than when he first got the toys, so he will look at them in a new light.

Your toddler may remember having played with a toy before. Or maybe he didn't even play with a particular toy six months or a year ago but now appreciates it. Or perhaps another toy is more fun now because your toddler knows more colors and shapes. Or maybe your toddler got bored with something a while back but may now find it intriguing once again. Maybe your toddler is old enough to understand that a particular toy was his as a baby and would find that interesting. With toddlers, you never know. So give it a try, and discover what your little one likes to rediscover.

Skills learned

Your toddler can learn anything a particular toy teaches, such as numbers, letters, colors, and shapes.

Make a craft box for all kinds of projects.

When you have a minute here and there, add something to a designated craft box. A plastic storage bin works well. Throw in anything that your little one will be able to use when making collages, picture frames, doorknob signs—anything.

Collect scraps of wrapping paper, ribbon, buttons, yarn, string, sequins, pom-poms, craft foam shapes, cotton, swatches of fabric, washable crayons and markers, construction paper, card stock, white paper, tissue paper, straws, paper cups, magazines, stickers, a washable-glue stick, and some tape, for example. Or when you happen to have one of these items out for a reason—after you receive a gift or when you buy a new bag of straws—stick a couple in the bin.

You will build up your supply in no time with virtually no extra effort. Then your toddler will have all these things on hand when he or she is feeling crafty. Just pull out the bin and let your toddler go crazy with crafts.

Skills learned

By having unlimited craft supply options, your toddler's artistic creations will be beyond limits. This will teach your child to think creatively and create no boundaries with his or her artwork.

4

Out and About

Children love playing outdoors. And with just a little bit of planning ahead, you can create several activities for your little one to do outside while you wash windows, rake leaves, sweep the porch, hang laundry, or work for your part-time job while sitting on a bench or at a table outside taking in the fresh air. The outdoor activities in this chapter require just fifteen minutes or less of preparation time and will really help you out.

Have your toddler glue sand and shells on cardboard to make a beach scene.

You will want to do this one outdoors. Cut a piece of cardboard or two. Put some sand in a paper or plastic bowl. Put some small shells in another bowl. Then give your toddler some liquid glue and let her squirt it all over the cardboard. Then briefly show your toddler what to do. Sprinkle a pinch of sand at a time over the glue and stick on some shells.

Your toddler will get the hang of it right away and can take over. You're outside, so let your child be what she wants to be—messy.

This project may be one that turns out even better when taken on by a child who may not be as concerned about natural tendencies of symmetry, patterns, or evenness. Let your toddler put a clump of shells in one corner if that's what she wishes. Have no rules; it's all right. Your little one also may glue on blue tissue paper for sky and cotton balls for clouds. Add glitter to the sand to give the picture an extra sparkle.

The more your little one does on her own, the better it will turn out.

Skills learned

Your child will learn something very important from making a sandy beach scene: the beauty of imperfection in nature and of all God's creatures.

Let your toddler pack and unpack for a picnic.

The first stage of this activity is done indoors. Grab a basket you may have lying around the house. It doesn't have to be a picnic basket. Then gather some paper or plastic bowls, plates and cups, and some napkins and plasticware. Put all the items on the table. Give the basket to your toddler and have him pack each picnic item. Have your child pack one plate for himself and one plate for you. If your little one cannot count two of each item, he can just pack whatever you get out. Also, you may want to let your toddler pack a couple of snacks from the pantry.

When it is time for his lunch, make a couple of sandwiches and head outside with a sheet or blanket. Spread it on a table or on the ground, and while you are taking care of an outdoor chore, your toddler can unpack the items and set up for a picnic lunch with Mom (or Dad). He even could practice pouring two drinks from a pitcher or plastic bottle, providing it is not too heavy. After all, a mess won't matter because you're outside.

Finally, when you're done with your task or your toddler is finished with picnic preparations, you can share the special lunch. Don't forget to say a blessing together.

Pursue righteousness, godliness, faith, love, endurance and gentleness.

1 Timothy 6:11

Skills learned

Your toddler can learn several skills by preparing for a picnic, including what items to bring on a picnic, how to set up on a blanket, hand-eye coordination as he practices pouring the drinks, and how to bless the food.

Tack paper to a tree and let your toddler paint on it.

Letting a toddler paint inside is probably a recipe for disaster. It can become more of a mess than it is worth if you're not right there by her side constantly.

However, if it's nice out and you have tasks to do outside or paperwork for a job that you can do sitting on a bench, painting is a good option. A mess outside probably is not a problem. So try tacking a large piece of paper to a tree and let the tree be your child's easel. Tack the top of the paper out of your child's reach, and you may want to secure the bottom with some tape to keep the paper in place.

Your toddler could use a paintbrush or finger paints. Of course, inside or out, washable paints are always a good idea; it makes cleaning clothing—and your child—easier. The bark may create an interesting texture on your toddler's painting. This activity surely will paint a lasting memory in your child's mind.

Skills learned

Your toddler can learn more about the outdoors and textures of tree bark while honing her painting skills in the fresh air.

Fill up the blow-up pool while you work outside.

Blow-up kiddie pools are underrated. If you have outdoor chores—maybe hanging laundry, pulling weeds, sweeping the porch, or cutting back rose bushes—set up the pool near you so you can keep an eye on your toddler splashing in the pool. He will love playing in the water, especially if it's hot outside. Don't forget to throw in beach balls, sand buckets, bath toys, or any other toys your toddler wants that can be immersed in water.

You're not only keeping your toddler occupied and happy—which is no small task—but you have now consolidated two activities—playtime and a chore or two—saving you time. And since playing outdoors makes kids sleepier, you may take advantage of nap time to accomplish some indoor chores or work. If you do not have a pool, you often can find them for ten dollars or less near the end of the warm-weather season.

Skills learned

By splashing around in a kiddie pool, your child can improve his balance in water and become more comfortable in a pool. This will help your little one to not be afraid when learning to swim some day in a grown-up pool.

Make homemade bubble stuff for your toddler.

Bubble-blowing is a timeless treasure for toddlers. There's something fascinating about creating seemingly gravity-defying air pockets from a cup of liquid. To make it, squirt some liquid dish soap and some water into a small plastic container and stir it. You can use empty plastic juice containers with screw-on caps—ten ounces is a good size.

Make sure you save any bubble wands you get from stores for future use with homemade bubbles. But if you don't have any on hand, you can make one by making a loop using a large paper clip or pipe cleaner, if your child can use it safely.

You can sit outside and do paperwork or other tasks related to your business while your child enjoys blowing bubbles time and time again.

Skills learned

Besides having a ball, your toddler will learn how to make bubble stuff and how to be patient and blow slowly to get the best results. This can teach him or her a lifelong lesson on the benefits of having patience.

Have your toddler make a collage using items found in nature.

The first step in this activity is a fun, wholesome event for you and your toddler together: going on a nature walk. Go while at the park or even out in your own backyard. Collect leaves, sticks, acorns, pine needles, ferns, flower petals, and anything else that your toddler can glue onto a collage.

Give your toddler some washable liquid school glue and a decent-sized piece of cardboard and let her make her own creation. For added beauty, tear up some squares of tissue paper and have your toddler glue them to the cardboard, covering the background, before beginning the collage.

You can tailor this project to the time of year. For example, in winter, you may want to use blue tissue paper for a wintry background, while ferns make nice Christmas trees. In summer, you could make a bright background in yellow or orange and use lots of greenery. Add any items you have around the house—such as cotton balls for snowmen or clouds—to enhance the collage.

Your toddler will want to stick to a fun project such as this one.

Tip

Since glue is useful for so many projects for toddlers, you may want to get a decent supply of it during stores' back-to-school sales.

Skills learned

By creating a nature collage, your little one will learn about the many different items found in nature.

Hand your toddler off to your spouse.

Virtually nothing is certain with a toddler. Your precious little toddler can change his mind from one minute to the next. Suddenly, your little one can lose interest in an activity without any notice or warning.

So when all else fails with keeping your toddler occupied, there's one sure cure that will remedy the situation: Give your little sweetie to your husband (or wife, if you're a stay-at-home dad) and have them go away. Far away. And lock the doors and don't let them back in for at least two hours.

Be nice to them, though. Even pack a care package with extra clothes, snacks, drinks, and a few toys, and send your spouse and your toddler on their way. The two of them can bond together at the park or at the zoo, for example. These opportunities will give you the time you need to work while building memories your spouse and toddler will treasure forever.

> If you call out for insight
>   and cry aloud for understanding,
> and if you look for it as for silver
>   and search for it as for hidden treasure,
> then you will understand the fear of the LORD
>   and find the knowledge of God.
> For the LORD gives wisdom,
>   and from his mouth come knowledge and understanding.

> Proverbs 2:3–6

Skills learned

This activity will let your child know how much Daddy (or Mommy) loves him. And this is the most important thing we can pass on to our children.

Tip

Never discount the power of prayer for guidance on how to handle a situation with your toddler. Pray for creativity, patience, imagination, and wisdom.

Melissa Bogdany *was managing editor, news editor, and reporter of a weekly business newspaper for eight years before becoming editor of* Christian Retailing *magazine. She decided to leave the corporate world when she became a mother and currently writes and edits from home while caring for her young daughter in Chuluota, Florida.*